"Starving Armenians"

"Starving

MERRILL D. PETERSON

Armenians"

America and the Armenian Genocide,
1915–1930 and After

University of Virginia Press Charlottesville and London

University of Virginia Press
© 2004 by the Rector and Visitors of the University of Virginia
All rights reserved
Printed in the United States of America on acid-free paper

First published 2004

9 8 7 6 5 4 3 2 1

LIBRARY OF CONGRESS CATALOGING-IN-PUBLICATION DATA
Peterson, Merrill D.
  "Starving Armenians" : America and the Armenian Genocide, 1915–1930
and after / Merrill D. Peterson.
    p.   cm.
Includes bibliographical references.
  ISBN 0-8139-2267-4 (cloth : alk. paper)
    1. Armenian massacres, 1915–1923—Foreign public opinion, American.
2. Genocide—Turkey—Foreign public opinion, American. I. Title.
DS195.5. P48 2004
956.6'2015—dc22

                                                                2003018274

Illustration sources can be found at the end of the book

TO THE MEMORY OF VICTIMS AND SURVIVORS

Contents

Illustrations

Preface

THE FIRST WORDS I remember my mother saying to me in the dim light of childhood were "Clean your plate! Think of the starving Armenians!" Some seventy years later, as I was preparing to go to Armenia for service in the Peace Corps, astonished friends and acquaintances exclaimed, "Armenia! All I know about Armenia is that my mother told me, 'Clean your plate! Think of the starving Armenians!'"

As I read at length about Armenia, an independent republic of three million people buried in the Transcaucasus—only recently freed from the grip of the Soviet Union—I became fascinated by the history and culture of this ancient people and its amazing powers of survival through centuries of persecution and oppression. The "starving Armenians" were the saving remnant of the genocide committed by the Ottoman Turks during the First World War. And so the riddle of my childhood gradually explained itself.

On Memorial Day 1997 I flew via Amsterdam to Yerevan, the capital of Armenia, with the new class of Peace Corps volunteers to that country. I brought with me a book just off the press, *Black Dog of Fate,* a memoir by the young poet and third-generation Armenian American Peter Balakian. Never did I employ a long flight to better advantage. Alas, my Peace Corps adventure ended in failure. My health did not hold up, and I was sent home.

After receiving my medical discharge, I wrote a little memoir, "My Six Weeks in the Peace Corps: An Armenian Adventure," published in the *Virginia Quarterly Review*. I supposed that was the end of it. But in the course of reading I became interested in the Holocaust, and this subject led me back to the Armenian genocide. By chance I came upon the burgeoning refugee problem of the World War era, and in this connection discovered the remarkable philanthropic work of the missionary-inspired organization that came to be called Near East Relief, which was principally responsible for saving the remnant of the genocide. The resulting diaspora, although worldwide, came to be centered in the United States. The Armenian story became warp and woof with the American story.

Acknowledgments

I OWE SPECIAL THANKS to the manuscript collections of a number of research libraries: the Library of Congress, the Houghton Library of Harvard University, the New York Public Library, and the Sophia Smith Collection of Smith College. State Department documents in the U.S. National Archives were a useful resource; and, as in the past, I have been sustained by the holdings and the services of the University of Virginia Library. A visit to the Armenian Library and Museum, in Watertown, Massachusetts, was enjoyable as well as rewarding. As before, Donna Packard was my proficient word-processor; and I again owe thanks to Barbara Salazar for her keenness and subtlety in copyediting my manuscript. Thanks are also due to Bill Abbot, my longtime friend and colleague, for reading the manuscript at an early stage. My cherished companion, Nini Almy, made invaluable contributions from beginning to end.

David Kherdian's "For My Father" is from *Homage to Adana* (Fresno: Giligia Press, 1971) and is reproduced here with his permission. An excerpt from William Saroyan's *Here Comes, There Goes, You Know Who* is reprinted with the permission of Simon & Schuster Adult Publishing Group, copyright © 1961 by Aram Saroyan and Lucy Saroyan. The last stanza of "The History of Armenia," from *June-Tree: New and Selected Poems, 1974–2000*, by Peter Balakian, is

"Starving Armenians"

Prologue: The Ambassador's Story

HENRY MORGENTHAU, newly appointed United States ambassador to the Ottoman Empire, sailed through the Golden Horn, where East meets West, to take up residence in the embassy at Constantinople in the fall of 1913. On the city's crowding hills rose the Byzantine palaces, the mosques and churches, the splendid monuments, the gilded domes and soaring minarets of the centuries-old capital. After two event-making years, Morgenthau would return to the United States as the man who alerted his country, indeed the world, to the barbaric crime committed by Turkey against the Armenian people in their midst.

When President Woodrow Wilson, newly elected, first proposed the Turkish post to Morgenthau, the finance chairman of the successful Democratic campaign, he had declined it. He preferred a policy-making place, perhaps at Treasury or Commerce, in the new administration. The present ambassador in Constantinople, Oscar S. Straus, whose Jewish father had emigrated to the United States from Germany, as Morgenthau himself had done, had served in the post for so long, under so many administrations, that it assumed the character of a Jewish fiefdom in the United States government, as if it were, said Morgenthau, "the only diplomatic post to which a Jew can aspire."[1] Wilson, in fact, wanted a Jew at that station because of the paramount importance of Palestine and its

1

Jewish colonists in the Ottoman Empire. American interests in the Near East still centered on the protection of Christian missionaries and affiliated schools, colleges, seminaries, and hospitals. But on the eve of the European war the empire was in turmoil from the Adriatic to the Caucasus and from the Euphrates to the Nile. In 1908 a party of "Young Turks," organized as the Committee of Union and Progress (CUP), deposed the autocratic sultan Abdul Hamid II and introduced parliamentary government under a reactivated constitution. "Turkey for the Turks" became the rallying cry of the nationalist revolution that rose up in succession to the dying multinational empire of the Sublime Porte. Many European Jews, meanwhile, inspired by Zionist aspirations for a national homeland, migrated to Palestine. Germany joined the race of the European powers to control the economic development of the Near East, and Emperor William II courted the favor of the CUP. In these circumstances, the State Department instructed Ambassador Straus to transfer his efforts from the protection of missionary endeavors and institutions to matters of economic development: railroad and oil concessions and advancement of commerce.[2]

Traveling in Europe in the summer of 1913, the fifty-seven-year-old Morgenthau, whose most striking feature was a trim Van Dyke beard, remained eager for a career in public service after making a fortune as a New York lawyer, banker, and real estate investor. In Paris he met with Ambassador Myron Herrick, who warmly advised him to take the Turkish post, and also with Stephen S. Wise, the charismatic rabbi of the Free Synagogue in New York, to which Morgenthau belonged. Wise was returning from a tour of Palestine, and he emphasized the service a man of Morgenthau's talents might render the Jews there from the only American seat of importance in the Near East. He was persuasive.

Upon returning home Morgenthau advised the president of his change of mind. The nomination went forward to the Senate and Morgenthau was quickly confirmed. During a leisurely Atlantic crossing in the fall, he became acquainted with a group of Protestant missionaries returning from leave to their duties in the Near East. "I had hitherto had a hazy notion that missionaries were sort of over-zealous advance agents of sectarian religion and that their principal activity was the proselytizing of believers in other faiths," the New Yorker later wrote of this encounter. "To my surprise and gratification, these men gave me a very different picture. They were, I discovered, in reality advance agents of civilization."[3] That proved a useful lesson for the new ambassador.

After presenting his credentials to the Porte and meeting Sultan Muhammad V, Abdul Hamid's younger brother and nominal successor, the new ambassador made acquaintance with the power behind the throne, the cabinet ministers Talaat, Enver, and Djemal, the oligarchic triumvirate of the CUP. Talaat, with the title of minister of the interior, was the ablest and the most powerful of the trio, Morgenthau would conclude. Enver, minister of war, formerly military attaché in Berlin, affected the dashing style of the German officer corps. He and Morgenthau often rode horseback together. On the walls of his office Enver hung portraits of Napoleon and Frederick the Great. Djemal, minister of marine, was the mildest of the triumvirs. Morgenthau could not help seeing these men in his own mind as political bosses on the model of Tammany Hall.[4]

While thus getting acquainted with the Young Turks, he introduced himself as well to the American community in Constantinople, especially the missionary-educators William W. Peet, the representative of the American Board of Commissioners for Foreign Missions; Dr. Caleb Frank Gates, president of Robert College; and Dr. Mary Mills Patrick, president of the Woman's College. The ambassador was struck by the anomalies of his position: "Here was I, a Jew, representing the greatest Christian nation of the world at the capital of the chief Mohammedan nation." In a speech before the Chamber of Commerce of Constantinople he left no doubt about his true mission. It was not about sewing machines, petroleum, and tobacco, though business could not be neglected. It was rather to make his embassy a salient of American civilization in the Near East. It was, he declared, "to foster the permanent civilizing work of the Christian missions, which so gloriously exemplified the American spirit at its best."[5]

The coming of the European war presented new challenges to the ambassador. German designs envisioned Turkey as a vassal state. "Deutschland über Allah" was the way an embassy aide put it.[6] The Germans quickly closed the Dardanelles, thus bottling up the Russian enemy, though not before Germany had sneaked two of its cruisers into the Black Sea. The Ottomans then abrogated the "capitulations," which were the treaty arrangements that protected foreigners and their enterprises by placing them under the jurisdiction of their own countries' legal systems and exempting them from Ottoman laws. The churches and colleges and other American institutions were thus placed in jeopardy. Then, in November, Turkey entered the war on the side of the Central Powers. Given its strategic position, it at once became the Reich's most valuable ally. Morgenthau began to see a good deal of the German ambassador, Hans von Wangenheim, an imposing cigar-smoking Prussian. The Turkish military establishment had been reorganized along German lines. Morgenthau was mistaken, however, in supposing that it was controlled by Berlin.[7] War broke out between the eastern empires in October. The sultan then proclaimed a jihad, a holy war against the infidel; and Morgenthau thought he saw Germany's hand in this appeal to religious hatred. Fortunately, although the proclamation reverberated in the mosques, it fizzled ingloriously. Yet, Morgenthau later wrote, "it started passions aflame that afterward spent themselves in the massacres of the Armenian and other subject peoples." Early in 1915 the Allied fleets attempted to force the straits at the Dardanelles and capture Constantinople. The campaign, with every promise of success, failed in March, however, and the subsequent attack on the Gallipoli peninsula met the same fate. Morgenthau wrote mournfully, "Had the Allied fleets once passed the defenses at the straits, the administration of the Young Turks would have come to a bloody end." The embassy aide Lewis Einstein added that "the main sufferers" of the defeat would be the Armenians.[8]

The Armenians, numbering over 2.5 million, were scattered throughout Asia Minor. Perhaps half lived in Russian Armenia, lodged in the Caucasus in the shadow of Mount Ararat, where Noah's Ark was said to have come to rest. A million inhabited the six "homeland" *vilayets* (provinces) on the tablelands of eastern Anatolia; others belonged to so-called Little Armenia, in ancient Cilicia, between the Taurus Mountains and the Mediterranean Sea; and a substantial colony of Armenians transacted most of the business of the great metropolis, Constantinople. The Armenians were Christians; Armenia, in fact, was the first nation, in 301 A.D., to adopt Christianity. They had been persecuted through the ages, yet they survived; and in the nineteenth century, responding to currents of modernity and availing themselves of the education offered by Christian missionaries, mainly from America, they became fore-runners of Westernization in the Near East. The Armenian massacres, as they were commonly called, had their startling beginning in 1894–95, during the reign of Abdul Hamid II, the Red Sultan, and went on sporadically for years, before and after the Young Turk revolution, which the Armenians had greeted with high hopes, only to see them utterly crushed in 1915.

Early in that year, Djevdet Bey, brother-in-law of Enver Pasha, the war minister, came to the eastern walled city of Van with a commission to annihilate the Armenians. They made up three-fifths of the inhabitants. Van was a pretty city on a lake and the home of a well-staffed Protestant mission with schools, a college, and a hospital. Feelings were tense because of the war. The Armenians were naturally drawn to the Russians, an Allied power, nearby in the Caucasus, while the Turks demanded their loyalty and their service. Hostilities broke out in April, after the withdrawal of Russian troops. The Armenians, behind the walls of the old city, came under fiery siege by the Turkish army. When the siege was lifted after twenty-seven days, most of the Armenians were dead. Van had become a Golgotha. The Russians returned with nothing to do but to clean up the place. According to Dr. Clarence Ussher, director of the hospital, they cremated 55,000 bodies.[9]

Comparatively few Armenians—a respectable few—died in battle during the war. Most were victims of a brutal system of murder known as "deportation," for which the war was a smoke screen. Typically, in one village after another, the gendarmes would go from house to house, confiscate any arms, and take off the men, allegedly for work details, then instruct the women and children to prepare for a journey on foot to some unnamed destination. The men, of course, never returned. They were beaten to death or hideously dispatched in more barbaric fashion. The women and children formed long caravans pointed in the general direction of the Syrian desert or the Mesopotamian valley. Across the ambassador's desk in Constantinople came reports from United States consuls, missionaries, and other eyewitnesses. (Morgenthau's Armenian dragoman, Arshag K. Schmavonian, translated those written in his own language.) As Morgenthau later described it:

> From thousands of Armenian cities and villages these despairing caravans now set forth; they filled all the roads leading southward; everywhere, as they moved on, they raised a huge dust, and abandoned debris, chairs, blankets, bedclothes, household utensils, and other impedimenta marked the course of the procession. When the caravans first started, the individuals bore some semblance to human beings; in a few days, however, the dust of the road plastered their faces and clothes, the mud caked their lower members, and the slowly advancing mobs, frequently bent with fatigue and crazed by

the brutality of the "protectors," resembled some new and strange animal species. Yet for the better part of six months, from April to October, 1915, practically all the highways in Asia Minor were crowded with these unearthly bands of exiles. . . . In these six months, as far as can be ascertained, about 1,200,000 people started on this journey.[10]

In June, Leslie Davis, consul at Harpoot, a city of 30,000 perched on a hill above the broad plain, wrote distressingly, "Another method has been found to destroy the Armenian race. This is no less than the deportation of the entire Armenian population . . . from all six vilayets. A massacre would be humane in comparison with it. In a massacre many escape, but a wholesale deportation of this kind in this country means a lingering and perhaps more dreadful death for nearly everyone."[11]

During the summer and fall shocking accounts of the massacres surfaced in American newspapers and magazines. "Armenian Horrors Grow" and "Tell of Horrors Done in Armenia" were among the headlines in the *New York Times*. Readers already emotionally drained by Belgian atrocities were scarcely prepared for something ten times worse. For some the stories smelled of Allied propaganda. But after James Bryce, the English author and statesman, former ambassador to the United States, made a dramatic and solidly based report in the House of Lords, Americans sat up and took notice. Bryce's authority was unimpeachable. Forty years earlier he had ascended Mount Ararat, then published a travel journal, *Transcaucasia and Ararat,* that practically introduced the Western mind to Armenia. In 1915 Bryce joined with a rising young historian, Arnold J. Toynbee, in compiling a pamphlet, *Armenian Atrocities.* The following year, at the request of the Foreign Office, he collaborated on a massive blue book, *The Treatment of the Armenians in the Ottoman Empire,* for civic enlightenment. In both Great Britain and the United States Armenian relief funds sprang up almost overnight.

Morgenthau, meanwhile, confronted the Young Turks with the evidence in his bulging Armenian file. They had, he believed with German prodding, revived Abdul Hamid's satanic enterprise of resolving the Armenian Question by exterminating the Armenians. In one of his interviews, Talaat freely conceded the point. The plan embodied in the deportations had been approved by the CUP after prolonged and careful consideration. "We have our objections to the Armenians on three distinct grounds," he told Morgenthau. "In the first place, they have enriched themselves at the expense of the Turks. In the second place, they are determined to domineer over us and to establish a separate state. In the third place, they have openly encouraged our enemies." The latter charge was based mainly on instances of aid to the Russians in the Caucasus, which Morgenthau had already dismissed as of small importance. "Why are you so interested in the Armenians anyway?" Talaat asked on another occasion. "You are a Jew; these people are Christians." Morgenthau replied, "You don't seem to realize that I am not here as a Jew but as the American Ambassador. My country contains something more than 97,000,000 Christians and something less than 3,000,000 Jews. So, at least in my ambassadorial capacity, I am 97 per cent Christian." Talaat objected to Americans' spending money for the relief of Armenians. Why don't you give it to us? he pleaded. One day he astonished the ambassador with a particularly callous request. He asked that American life insurance companies that had written policies for the Armenians be directed to make the Ottoman government their beneficiary. "They are practically all dead now and have left no heirs to collect the money. It of course all escheats to the State." Morgenthau was left speechless.[12]

The ambassador opened a back channel through the German embassy to exert pressure on the Turkish ally to stop the massacres, apparently without success. As Lewis Einstein observed, "The Germans, to their eternal disgrace, will not lift a finger to save the Armenians." Their responsibility, it seems, was not in instigating and abetting the crime, as Morgenthau inclined to believe, but in doing nothing to arrest it. Wangenheim, in poor health, categorically refused to intervene; and after a heated encounter with Morgenthau in October 1915, he retired to home and bed and suffered a fatal stroke. Morgenthau found a strong mind and a sympathetic ear in Dr. Johannes Lepsius, a representative of German missionary interests and long a friend of Armenia. Lepsius, having been given free range in Morgenthau's file, diligently pursued his search for evidence, and upon his return to Berlin launched a campaign implicating the German Reich in the Armenian massacres. His published indictment deeply embarrassed the Wilhemstrasse. While Germany stood by, half the Armenian nation was annihilated. "Our conscience demands the rescue of the other half." With that Lepsius prudently chose to cross the border into Holland.[13]

Morgenthau was in regular communication with the State Department about the Armenian catastrophe from April 27, 1915. At first, of course, it was not clear that it was a catastrophe. The CUP leaders seemed to be responding to revolutionary elements among the Armenians; and Morgenthau conjectured that that campaign would be followed by action against Zionist Jews. By July, however, an annihilative assault on the Armenian people was clear. "Reports from widely scattered districts," he cabled, "indicate systematic attempt to uproot peaceful Armenian population and through arbitrary arrests, terrible torture, wholesale expulsions and deportation from one end of the Empire to the other, accompanied by frequent instances of rape, pillage, and murder, turning into massacre, to bring destruction and destitution on them." The movement was wholly under civil authority. It was not in response to popular or fanatical demand; nor could it be justified in the name of wartime security and defense, despite the lame excuse of treachery on the Russian border. The ambassador explained the protests he had lodged with the ministers and the grand vizier, and asked for guidance on drawing the line between expressions of humanitarian concern and interference in internal affairs. He was growing frustrated by the failure of the United States government to respond in a positive way to the crisis. "I earnestly beg the Department to give this matter urgent and exhaustive consideration." What was at stake was the survival of a people almost as old as human history. Could not a weighty protest be lodged? And could not every facility be given to aid and rescue the sufferers?[14]

In a cable dated September 3, 1915, Morgenthau made an unusual request to the secretary of state. "Will you," he asked, "suggest to Cleveland Dodge, Charles Crane, John R. Mott, Stephen Wise, and others to form committees to raise funds and provide means to save some of the Armenians and assist the poorer ones to emigrate?"[15] The message was forwarded to James L. Barton, secretary of the American Board of Commissioners for Foreign Missions, in Boston. Barton himself had once been a missionary in the Near East. He was one of the group Morgenthau had met on his voyage to Europe two years before. Seizing the critical moment, Barton sent out calls for a meeting, September 16, in the office of the New York businessman-philanthropist Cleveland H. Dodge. The meeting led to the formation of the Armenian Relief Committee under Barton's chairmanship. Several members of the board of trustees, among them Dodge, a mining company executive, were personal friends of President Wilson. Nearly all had long experience in American educational and religious efforts in the Near East. Dodge's children were conspicuous in this regard. Before it adjourned the organization set an emergency goal of $100,000. This amount, half of it the gift of the Rockefeller Foundation, was promptly dispatched to Ambassador Morgenthau—a down payment on the millions the organization would eventually raise.[16]

A front-page story in the *New York Times* on October 4 described the Armenian atrocities in heartbreaking detail. Uprooted mothers abandoned their infants in the desert or tossed them into the Euphrates to drown; girls were ravished or sold to become Muslims;

men were tortured with the bastinado and other brutalities in the course of massacre; all were starving to death.[17] Two weeks later a great rally took place in the Century Theatre, on Central Park West, addressed by Barton, Hamilton Holt, editor of the *Independent,* Rabbi Wise, and the stem-winder W. Bourke Cochran, among others. Relief committees earlier formed joined forces with this impressive new organization. It evolved through several changes of name to become known finally and definitively as Near East Relief, 70 Fifth Avenue, New York.

In February 1916 Morgenthau returned to the United States, technically on leave; but his tour of duty in Constantinople was over. He said that Turkey had become "a place of horror" for him, and he could no longer bear dealing with the men who "were still reeking with the blood of nearly a million human beings." He wished also to work for the reelection of President Wilson. Nothing in international politics was more important than that, he believed. In a departing interview with Talaat, the ambassador made a final appeal on behalf of the Armenians. "What's the use of speaking about them?" Talaat retorted. "We are through with them. That's all over." The only hope for them, Morgenthau had come to believe, was "the moral power of the United States."[18] Wilson was necessary to that project. So was the mobilization of American aid and opinion under the leadership of Barton and Dodge and their associates. "City Rises to Honor Henry Morgenthau," read the *Times* headline on his arrival in New York Harbor. His book *Ambassador Morgenthau's Story* appeared two years later.

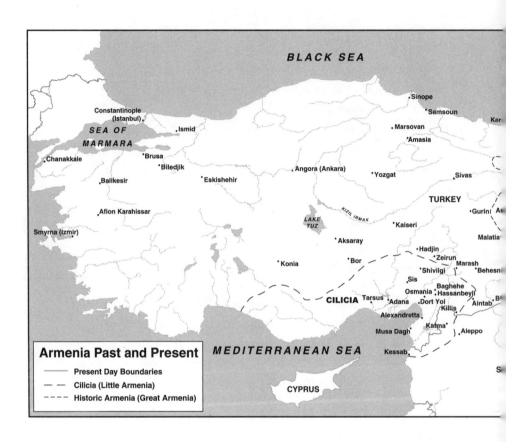

Armenia Past and Present

——— Present Day Boundaries
— — Cilicia (Little Armenia)
- - - - Historic Armenia (Great Armenia)

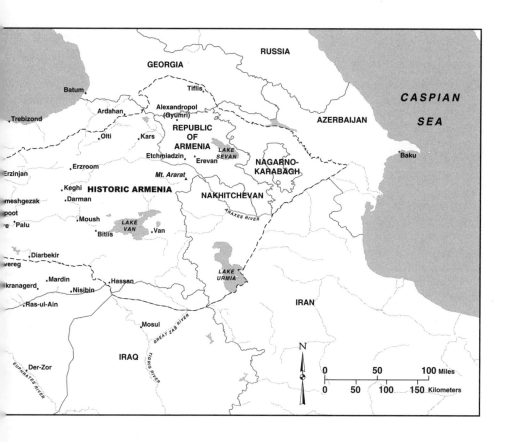

RUSSIA

GEORGIA

CASPIAN
SEA

Batum

Tiflis

Trebizond

Ardahan

Alexandropol
(Gyumri)

AZERBAIJAN

Olti

Kars

REPUBLIC
OF
ARMENIA

Baku

Erzjnjan

Erzroom

Etchmiadzin

Erevan

LAKE
SEVAN

NAGARNO-
KARABAGH

Keghi

HISTORIC ARMENIA

Mt. Ararat

NAKHITCHEVAN

meshgezak

poot

Darman

e Palu

Moush

LAKE
VAN

Van

ARAXES RIVER

Bitlis

Diarbekir

vereg

LAKE
URMIA

kranagerd

Mardin

Hassan

Nisibin

IRAN

Ras-ul-Ain

Mosul

N

Der-Zor

IRAQ

GREAT ZAB RIVER

TIGRIS RIVER

EUPHRATES RIVER

0   50   100 Miles

0   50   100   150 Kilometers

1 | *Awakening*

THE ARMENIANS WERE AN ancient Indo-European people who had inhabited the highlands of eastern Anatolia since the ninth century B.C. Herodotus said they had come from Phrygia, below the Black Sea, far to the west. More recent historians trace them to the Iron Age kingdom of Urartu, in the vicinity of Lake Van. Situated on the land bridge between Europe and Asia, Armenia lay in the path of conquerors—Greek, Persian, Roman. Only briefly, in the first century B.C., under Tigranes the Great, was it an independent kingdom. Centuries of oppression and persecution followed. Armenia became a Christian island in a sea of Islam. In the fifteenth century it was absorbed into the rising Ottoman Empire, which had swept away Byzantium.

Armenia emerged as an issue and a problem in international politics coincident with the Eastern Problem during the latter half of the nineteenth century. This was the problem of Turkey, "the Sick Man of Europe" in Western eyes, and of the declining Ottoman Empire. Beginning with Greece in 1832, one country after another gained its independence and fell away. Increasingly Turkey lagged badly and behaved badly by European standards, yet proved resistant to reform. Increasingly Armenians bore the brunt of Turkish transgressions. These were first dramatized, however, in Bulgaria in 1876, when Turkish fears of revolt by a subject people led to the massacre of some ten thousand Bulgarians. The repressive measures drew from William Gladstone, the British liberal statesman, a denunciation that shook the chancelleries of Europe and echoed around the world. Gladstone lifted "the Bulgarian horrors" above mere politics and diplomacy to the lofty moral plane of humanity and civilization.[1]

Armenia was not yet an issue, but the boiling crisis in the Balkans raised apprehensions over the fate of Christian minorities whether in European Turkey or in the Near East. In 1876 a young sultan, Abdul Hamid II, ascended the throne in Constantinople, and in a nod to liberalism he granted Turkey its first constitution. The calming effect of the gesture quickly passed; and the following year the Russian tsar, Alexander II, declared war on the Ottoman Empire. The war blew the lights out of the empire in the Balkans and led to Russian conquests in eastern Anatolia. The humiliating peace treaty, signed under the nose of the Sublime Porte at San Stefano, secured the independence of Serbia, Romania, and Montenegro, along with autonomy for Bulgaria, and ceded to Russia important cities, ports, and territories inhabited by Armenians. The terms of the accord created uneasiness among European powers, most especially Great Britain, where it provided yet another set piece in the historic clash between Gladstone and Benjamin Disraeli, the reigning prime minister. He, backed by the queen, was a friend of Turkey and the enemy of Russia. The upshot of the clamor was the Congress of Berlin in 1878. The treaty signed there by the great powers did not reverse Turkey's fortunes, but it redrew the map of Europe in ways that better served everyone's selfish interests than the San Stefano accord. Here, at Berlin, Armenia made its debut on the stage of international politics. Its delegates, who sought autonomy for the eastern provinces of Anatolia, were but silent witnesses to the proceedings, of course. Returning to their homeland, the delegates could take little comfort in the one provision of the Treaty of Berlin that concerned the Armenians. Article 61 read:

The Sublime Porte undertakes to carry out, without further delay, the improvements and reforms demanded by local requirements in the provinces inhabited by Armenians, and to guarantee their security against Circassians and Kurds. It will periodically make known the steps taken to this effect to the powers, who will superintend its application.[2]

The article was so limp as to be worthless against the Sublime Porte. Nor did it make an impression on warlike Kurds and Circassians. It was a fraud, a piece of diplomatic artifice. Its only value, as the future would show, was as a standing reminder of a pledge once made but never, even in the most perilous times, meant to be fulfilled by the six signatory powers.

People looking to locate Armenia on a map were likely to be perplexed. It did not exist as a geographical entity. This anomaly gave rise to locutions like "provinces inhabited by Armenians," as in the Berlin treaty. It was less a place than a historic conception. There was, of course, Russian Armenia, wedged between the eastern Anatolian highlands and the Transcaucasus. The province had been taken from Persia by conquest in 1828, and although it was inhabited by Armenians—many of them having fled Turkish rule—it was a Russian domain. (It appears, with some boundary modifications, on today's map as an independent country.) Greater Armenia, sometimes called the "Homeland," extended from Samsoun below the coastline of the Black Sea to Batum, inland from near Sivas to the Euphrates River, and easterly to Lake Van and Mount Ararat. Southward, across the Taurus Mountains to Adana and the Gulf of Alexandretta, lay Cilicia, sometimes called Little Armenia, which traced its founding back to 1080.

Accurate population figures are hard to come by. But the patriarch of the Apostolic Church placed the total Armenian population at 2.6 million in 1882.[3] Well over a majority of the people were scattered through the countless towns and communities of the six "homeland" vilayets, or provinces: Erzroom, Van, Bitlis, Harpoot, Diarbekir, and Sivas. Most of the people were peasants who scratched out a frugal life in a forbidding environment. Only in Van did the Armenians constitute something like a majority of the population. For they lived among Turks and Kurds, both Muslim, and under this "double yoke," as one observer named it, the Armenians grew increasingly restless.[4] They were a religious as well as an ethnic minority. Great Russia claimed over a million Armenians, Cilicia counted something under 400,000. Approximately 7 percent of the total population, or 180,000, lived in Constantinople. They represented the wealth and the power of the people. They were the Armenian bourgeoisie, the merchants and bankers, and they filled the upper ranks of the Ottoman civil service. Charles Eliot, secretary of the British Embassy toward the end of the century, took an astute, if unflattering, view of the Armenian character. They were, he said, "a race with little political aptitude or genius for kingdom-building," yet, he conceded, "a people of great commercial and financial talents, supple and flexible as those must be who wish to make others part with their money: stubborn to heroism in preserving certain characteristics, but wanting withal in the more attractive qualities, in artistic sense, kindliness, and some (though not all) forms of courage."[5]

A perspicacious British traveler in Armenia during the 1890s wrote, "When one reflects upon the social conditions of the country no circumstance is perhaps more striking than the complete separation of one race from another. Although living side by side, there is an entire absence of natural fusion of the different elements upon a common plane."[6] Turk, Kurd, and Armenian—to say nothing of Circassian—differed in so many ways and spoke different languages. The written Armenian language was the creation of the scribe Mesrop-Mashtots, in 405, a century after Gregory the Illuminator established the church. An alphabet of thirty-six letters mimicked the sounds of ordinary speech. The written language, like the church, contributed to a unique culture and to the perpetuation of Armenian nationality against every exertion opposing it. Educated Armenians knew Turkish and Kurdish as well, though few Turks and Kurds knew Armenian. The Armenians were a civilized people long before the Osmanli, or Ottoman, Turks had been heard of. In the Middle Ages, Armenian builders of churches and monasteries made important architectural innovations; monks labored to engrave on parchment and paper brilliant illuminated manuscripts that, while indebted to Byzantine and Persian art, were a creation apart. The nineteenth century witnessed a renaissance of Armenian literature, exemplified in the prolific work of the nationalist and revolutionary author Raffi, whose identity was absorbed into his pen name. He lived and worked in Tiflis, the Georgian capital, and it was from there that much art and enlightenment came to the Armenians.

Another and very different source of enlightenment came through the American Protestant missionary movement in Turkey. In 1830 two young Congregational ministers, Eli Smith and Harrison Gray Otis Dwight, sailed some 6,000 miles from Boston to Constantinople, then journeyed deep into the Turkish interior to survey the prospects for evangelization in this distant land. Upon their return the travelers wrote a two-volume work, *Researches . . . in Armenia* (1833), in which it was said, "of America, they [the Armenians] had never heard under any name." Numbers of missionaries began arriving in the 1830s and swelled twenty years later. They were of various denominations, but the main stream was Congregationalist, fed by the American Board of Commissioners for Foreign Missions in Boston. While they ministered among other peoples in the Near East—Assyrians, for instance—some 90 percent of their work was among Armenians. By 1900, some three hundred missionaries labored in 162 missions from twenty-one stations, most of them equipped with hospitals.[7]

At first notice it is strange that Americans chose to evangelize among Christians in another land. But in Islam apostasy was a capital offense. So when Muslim Turks turned a deaf ear to their gospel, the missionaries found a warm reception among the searching Armenians. Many were dissatisfied with the traditional liturgy of the Gregorian church. Their displeasure had nothing to do with the church's doctrine of Monophysitism, positing the single divine nature of Christ, upon which it had maintained its independence from both Catholic and Orthodox communions for many centuries. It had to do, rather, with the teaching of a gospel they found more spiritually uplifting. The Armenian Apostolic Church, like the Greek Orthodox, had not experienced the Protestant Reformation and so had little knowledge of the evangelical message of redemption through faith rather than through works. As one of the missionary family wrote, the missionaries "recognized the essential Christian character of the [Armenian] churches, and their object was to set before them not a new creed or a different form of church government, but simply a higher conception of what constituted Christian life."[8] The missionaries translated the New Testament into the Armeno-Turkish vernacular and taught what seemed like "a new religion that was simple and understandable," in the words of one convert, who worried that, by seeming to deny the old church, conversion degraded his nationality.[9]

If these restless souls were to make the most of the new gospel, they must be better educated. This was axiomatic among the missionaries. And so they began schools and seminaries and colleges, and set their printing presses humming with writings both sacred and secular. Education, in turn, nurtured the rising political consciousness of the people as the century drew to a close. Edwin Pears, the distinguished British correspondent in Constantinople, wrote in his recollections that the missionaries became "the schoolmasters" of the country and "in a very real sense . . . the fomenters of political agitation in Armenia."[10]

These American missionaries were a hardy and stubborn breed. Elias Riggs went to Turkey in 1830 after graduating from Amherst College, and he spent sixty-eight years in the service. His children and grandchildren faithfully followed in his footsteps. Mr. and Mrs. George Cushing Knapp, newly married, joined a group of seven evangelists bound for the Near East in 1855. They settled on a high plateau above the valley of the Bitlis River where it cut an avenue into the Mesopotamian plains. A son, George Perkins Knapp, Harvard '87, succeeded his father at Bitlis. His bride was a Mount Holyoke graduate. Sixteen years later two sisters, Charlotte and Mary Ely, also graduates of that college, started Mount Holyoke Seminary in Bitlis, dedicated to the education of Armenian women. It adopted the motto of the founders' alma mater: "That our daughters may be as corner stones, polished after the similitude of the palace." Perhaps no missionary had a more illustrious career in the Near East than Caleb Frank Gates. A graduate of Beloit College, in Wisconsin, he went out in 1881; some years later he became president of Euphrates College, in Harpoot, a mission center, and later still of Robert College in Constantinople.[11] The first English college in the Near East, Robert was the gift of an American businessman and philanthropist, Christopher Robert; it opened its doors to students in 1863. Three years thence the Syrian Protestant College, later renamed the American University Beirut, came on the scene. Finally, to complete the constellation, the Constantinople Woman's College opened in 1871. None of these institutions owed their existence to the American Board, yet they were jewels in the crown of Protestant missionary endeavor in Turkey.

When a people heretofore powerless discover that they have become a pawn on the board of international politics, as did the Armenians in 1878, they are likely to become politically conscious in a hurry. The first sign of organized opposition to Abdul Hamid's autocratic regime came from Erzroom and called itself Defenders of the Fatherland. It was quickly and ruthlessly broken up. Two revolutionary parties, plugged into the currents of European socialism and nationalism, soon rose in its place. One, the Hunchak, after *hnchak,* meaning "bell" in Armenian, was avowedly socialist. It was formed in Geneva, that haven of revolutionary exiles, and appropriately took the name of the celebrated journal published there by the Russian revolutionary Alexander Herzen. The second, the Dashnak (federation), followed in 1890. It evolved into the Armenian Revolutionary Federation and became the spearhead of Armenian nationalism.[12] Other Christian minorities within the Ottoman Empire, such as the Serbs, had had powerful sponsors of their suits for independence, in this case Russia. Armenia did not. Meanwhile, the dynamics of the social situation in Anatolia, with a despotic ruler and a backward people on the one hand and a progressive and rapidly modernizing yet subject people on the other hand, were inherently unstable. The cultural gap between ruler and ruled, quite aside from the unbridgeable religious divide, bred envy, malice, and fear on a scale that could not be resolved or contained within the empire.

One solution to the problem was to rid the country of the Armenians. It must have occurred to Abdul Hamid, for his hatred of the Armenians was unbounded. Upon becoming sultan he had briefly submitted to parliamentary government, in which the Armenians, with other minorities, might have found a voice; but he then hastily reverted to absolutism. The sultan was intolerant of anything he could not understand or control. He had a morbid fear of sedition and insurrection, especially among the Armenians, and his spies alerted him to every supposed danger. Edwin Pears wrote of Abdul Hamid, "He is a man of a certain amount of cunning, but also of a meanness of character which is not Turkish." The journalist, with others speculating on the cause of the sultan's deep-dyed enmity to the Armenians, alluded to the rumor that his mother was of that people. "He was often spoken of as an Armenian or a half Armenian, and as these epithets undoubtedly came to his ear, they are probably one of the reasons which caused him to become bitterly hostile to the Armenian race."[13] Whatever may have been the psychic roots of this hatred, it seems clear that Abdul Hamid sought to deal with the Armenian problem by instruments of massacre and terror.

A favored instrument was the Kurds, who, it was said, alternately worshiped Allah and the Devil. The sultan armed the nomadic tribesmen and formed them into cavalry regiments, the Hamidieh, turned out smartly in Cossack-like uniforms. The Armenians were denied arms. Their relations with the Kurds were sometimes friendly, sometimes not. Late in the summer of 1894, at Sassoun, a mountainous area near Bitlis, Kurdish bands, joined by the Hamidieh, engaged in collecting an annual tax or tribute levied on the Armenians' crops and cattle. This time they were, surprisingly, met by resistance. The peasants, of course, paid lawful taxes to the government and objected to the Kurdish brigandage as a double tax. But in the palace at Constantinople the uprising was interpreted as an insurrection, and regular troops were sent to quell it. It became, in sum, a pretext to slaughter Armenians. Fighting went on for three weeks. The Armenian death toll was estimated as high as three thousand. "The Sassoun massacre," says a leading scholar, Vahakn N. Dadrian, "was the first instance of organized mass murder of Armenians in modern Ottoman history."[14] The sultan was compelled to accept an investigation by the signatory powers of the Berlin treaty, but it came to nothing.

A succession of massacres followed over the next two years. In September 1895 the Hunchak party organized an inflammatory demonstration at the very door of the Sublime Porte in Constantinople. It was accompanied by a "protest-demand" circulated among the embassies and the press. "Public opinion in Turkey," said Pears, "could hardly be said at any time to have existed outside Constantinople." Reason enough for the demonstration there. The protest was a plea for the end of persecution and oppression, for freedom and equality, and for recognition of the Armenians' "right to aspire to and to reach the level of progress and civilization towards which other people are advancing."[15] As death stalked the streets, thousands of Armenians took refuge in their churches. When the sultan made a gesture of conciliation, the protesters claimed victory and called off the demonstration. Meanwhile, in the eastern provinces, the massacres continued. At Trebizond, the ancient citadel above the Black Sea, Erzroom, Sivas, Diarbekir, and other places, the "autumn killings" went forward. Farther south, in Urfa, the cruelest of all the outrages occurred. On a Sunday three thousand Armenians retreated to the sanctuary of their great church; but the mob broke down the doors, shot and slashed randomly, then upon withdrawing set fire to the church with all its occupants.[16] Eight months later, in August 1896, Armenian revolutionaries of the Dashnak party captured the world's attention by seizing control of the Ottoman Bank in the capital. The bank was the financial heart of the empire and the manager of a huge public debt in which Western capitalists were heavily invested. For thirteen hours a small group of frightened and armed men barricaded themselves inside the bank. They, too, submitted demands, but almost as quickly gave themselves up to the authorities in exchange for their freedom to leave the country. As they sailed away to France, the historian Christopher Walker has written, "their fellow Armenians were left to expiate—many times over—the 'crime' of terrorizing a terrorist society." Two days of Turkish butchery and looting in the streets and along the fashionable avenues followed the Dashnaks' departure. Five to six thousand people were estimated to have lost their lives, most of them Armenians.[17]

With this spectacular incident the Hamidean massacres came to a close. They did not quite rise to the level of "genocide," as that term would later be defined; but they were, most surely, stepping-stones to the genocide yet to come. They created a "culture of massacre," as Dadrian has called it; and he places the total number of Armenian victims at 250,000.[18] That was the greater crime. To it may be added the lesser crimes of the European powers who had assumed a responsibility toward the Armenians but declined to intervene on their behalf and let the massacres go unpunished, unrepented, and unacknowledged.

The Hamidean massacres made the American people conscious of the Armenians and the Armenian Question for the first time. The Sassoun bloodbath was a front-page story in the *New York Times* and some other newspapers.[19] Mass meetings—one of two thousand people in Chicago—denounced the "Terrible Turk" and pledged aid and support to the Armenians. Churches conducted "Armenian Sundays." A national relief effort was mounted. The Reverend Edwin M. Bliss, son of a missionary family, published a book, *Turkey and the Armenian Atrocities,* profusely illustrated, introduced by Frances E. Willard, and intended to educate the American people on the subject. Beginning in February 1895 many Americans followed with interest the case of the missionary George P. Knapp, of Bitlis, accused of sedition by the Ottoman government. He could not be tried in a Turkish court because of the capitulations, but he was expelled. (Knapp lived to return to service and died a victim of the violence at Harpoot in 1915.) In retrospect, Americans' response was a rehearsal for their reaction to the genocide of 1915.

The response culminated in the mission of mercy of the American Red Cross under its head, Clara Barton, in 1895–96. She had been requested by the American Board to undertake relief in Turkey. Concerned to protect the neutral character of her organization internationally and wondering where the money would come from, Barton at first expressed reluctance. But the indignant response to the Armenian catastrophe in public meetings across the country changed her mind. The resident Turkish minister to the United States then declared she would not be admitted.

Nonetheless, typically intrepid, Barton gathered a small corps of workers and embarked for Turkey early in the new year. She met further resistance from the Sublime Porte, where it was insisted that any American relief must be distributed by Turkish hands. This obstacle, too, was overcome. The first well-stocked aid mission was sent by coastal boat to Alexandretta, in Cilicia, where famine and epidemic raged. During six months, aided by small miracles, workers spread out to Harpoot and Samsoun and elsewhere. Not only did the mission save lives, but it was a shot in the arm for American missionaries.[20]

Not many Americans at the end of the nineteenth century had ever met an Armenian in the flesh. Legend had it that one of that nationality had come to Virginia in the seventeenth century to engage in silkworm culture. But the Armenians scarcely figured in the rising flow of American immigration before 1890. Thereafter, and especially after 1895, their number rose dramatically. A total of 15,913 arrived in the United States in 1898, apparently as a result of the recent slaughter. From 1899 to 1917, 55,000 more came. The largest number settled in Massachusetts and New York. Often the immigrants took a long time to reach their destination. William Saroyan later told the story of the two-year passage of his grandmother and her family from Bitlis to New York, with repeated stops to work and earn money along the way. Not less important than the rising numbers was the quality of the Armenian immigrants. Statistics of the Immigration Bureau early in the twentieth century disclosed a higher percentage of skilled laborers and professionals among the Armenians than in any other ethnic group from southern Europe and Asia. They also enjoyed higher literacy (77 percent) and higher incomes than comparable ethnic groups. As a group they were comparatively well organized by means of national churches and benevolent associations. The latter funneled aid back to the homeland. And so it would later be said that no group or organization helped the Armenians as much as they helped each other. The newcomers brought Hunchak and Dashnak or other political loyalties with them. Through their newspapers they kept abreast of events in the homeland and, once settled, made substantial remittances to those left behind.[21]

According to the United States Census of 1920, 29 percent of the Armenian immigrants were naturalized citizens.[22] And so the Armenian story became part of the American story. The Hai, as the Armenians called themselves, brought a distinctive character to the American mix, one sometimes summed up in the word "grit." Their physical features—dark hair and eyes, prominent nose, firm and condensed build—seemed in accord with this character. Osip Mandelstam, the great Russian poet, described the Armenian language (Hayeran) as "prickly." That adjective might also apply to the Armenian character. Mandelstam liked the people. "The Armenian fullness of life," he would write in 1930, "their rough tenderness, their noble inclination to hard work, their inexplicable aversion to any kind of metaphysics, and their splendid intimacy with the world of real things—all this said to me: you're awake, don't be afraid of your own time, don't be shy."[23]

2 | Genocide

In 1908 a secret society of Young Turks, backed by an army corps in Salonika, dispatched an ultimatum to Sultan Abdul Hamid II demanding restoration of the abortive constitution of 1876. The sultan had no choice but to comply. At the same time, however, he plotted a counterrevolution, and this resulted in his overthrow a year later. The Committee of Union and Progress (CUP), as the executive arm called itself, combined European revolutionary idealism with profound disappointment over the deterioration of the Ottoman Empire. Armenians, led by the Dashnak rebels, were ecstatic and rushed to join the movement. They had for so long looked in vain for European intervention to aid their cause; now, it seemed, they might be able to help themselves. Hundreds of Armenian revolutionists returned from Russia. Fourteen Armenians found seats in the new parliament.

Armenia's euphoria soon went up in smoke. In 1909 the nation's penchant for human catastrophe rose again, this time at Adana, the ancient city on the fertile Cilician plain. No one understood who or what exactly provoked this massacre. But turbulence was in the air. There was from the first an element of Pan-Turkism—of strident Turkish nationalism—in the Young Turk revolution, and it may have lain behind the deadly uprising that began in Adana and spread like wildfire through the villages of the surrounding countryside.

As usual, the Armenians were the principal victims. The death toll was placed at upwards of 20,000. "Cilicia is destroyed," wrote a young Armenian author, Zapel Esayan, sent by the patriarch to investigate the outrage, and she later composed its epitaph in *Amid the Ruins.*[1] Perhaps it is the alliteration of the words that has led some historians to name the tragedy the "Cilician Vespers," after the Sicilian Vespers of 1282. One was a revolt of Sicilians seeking and securing independence from foreign domination, while the other was an atrocity committed against a people striving for freedom and human dignity, but instead rewarded with death or penury.

Adana marked the beginning of Armenian disillusionment with the Young Turks and their revolution. As the CUP sought to consolidate its power, the empire's disintegration continued apace. Bulgaria won its independence in 1908; the next year Austria annexed Bosnia-Hercegovina; Crete was finally lost to Greece; Tripoli, on the Mediterranean Sea, part of the empire with but one interruption since the sixteenth century, was conquered by Italy; and Albania, the last European outpost of the empire, proclaimed its independence in 1912. In the view of Robert Melson, "When by 1912 the CUP had lost control over nearly half of the Ottoman Empire's former territory, its leaders abandoned liberal Ottomanism and turned to a narrow chauvinistic and xenophobic Turkish nationalism, one of whose variations was Pan-Turkism."[2] The implications of this nationalism for Armenia's status as a millet, a non-Muslim community accorded religious autonomy within the empire, were especially troublesome.

The tsar's attack on Turkey in November 1914 ended any suspense that may have remained over its position in the enveloping European war. Turkey's contribution to the cause of the Central Powers consisted less in military victories than in presenting itself as a strategic obstacle to the Entente from the Dardanelles to the Caucasus. The Allies' support of Russia was thus seriously handicapped. And the Berlin to Baghdad Railroad, built with Turkish muscle and mostly German money, promised to open to the Reich a passageway to India.

Internally, the war offered a convenient cover for the genocide of the Armenians. When after the Second World War the crime of the intentional extermination of a racial, religious, or ethnic group found embodiment in the United Nations Genocide Treaty, historians soon realized that the term "genocide" perfectly fitted the crime against the Armenians in the First World War, and so it entered into the literature on that subject. In 1915 other and vaguer terms, such as "massacre," "atrocity," and "deportation," were commonly employed. (The Armenian word for it, *egherni,* meant slaughter.) But the lack of historicity of the noun "genocide" in 1915 should not now bar its usage in describing the terrible events of that time. Indeed, not to use this word may imply denial or avoidance of the true character of these events.

The beginnings of the genocide were virtually simultaneous with Turkey's entrance into the war, as if the two things were waiting for each other. Enver Pasha, secretary of war in the ruling triumvirate at Constantinople, took personal command of the Ottoman Third Army in the Caucasus, and in deep winter undertook to cut the Russian rail links to Turkey at a place called Sarikamish. Met with disastrous defeat, Enver reportedly blamed disloyal Armenian volunteers under his command. The cry of "Armenian treachery" was a hollow excuse for slaughter. Already orders had gone out from Constantinople to attack Armenian settlements in eastern Anatolia. Kurds joined in this work. Many villagers fled to Urmia, across the Persian border, where there was an important American mission. Others poured into Etchmiadzin, the holy city of the Gregorian church near Erivan. The gallant Armenian defense of Van has already been touched upon. On April 19, 1915, Djevdet Bey issued an order: "The Armenians must be exterminated. If any Muslim protect a Christian, first, his house shall be burnt; then the Christian killed before his eyes, then his [the Mus-

An Armenian family of Van

Refugees at Van crowding around a public oven, hoping to get bread

lim's] family and himself."[3] Meanwhile, at Zeitun, a medieval town perched in the Taurus Mountains, very largely Armenian in composition, the first of the deportations was launched in April. At Constantinople, Armenian officials in the Ottoman government were dismissed from their posts and with other leading figures— merchants, educators, writers, lawyers—sent into the interior, whence few returned. The exile peaked on April 24, the date that has become the annual day of mourning and remembrance among Armenians worldwide.[4]

These widely scattered events lacked the regularity of a system, and so might not, in themselves, qualify as a genocide. Talaat, at the head of the Central Committee of the CUP, took charge of the "Special Organization," as it was named, to carry out the "deportations," the euphemism for the murder and elimination of the Armenians. In place of wasteful and anarchic massacres, a plan was devised to accomplish the objective efficiently, systematically, with minimum jeopardy to the perpetrators, and virtually without cost. In the spring of 1915 a proclamation was drafted, printed, and ordered to be posted and cried out wherever Armenians lived in Turkey. A preamble declared that the Armenians had for many years imbibed from foreigners "a lot of false ideas of a nature to disturb the public order," and so had brought about "bloody happenings" subversive of the peace and good order of the state. They had now, moreover, sided with the enemy. For these reasons, the document went on, "the Armenians have to be sent away to places which have been prepared in the interior vilayets." The announcement then enjoined the following rules:

- First, all Armenians, saving the sick, are obliged within five days to leave their villages or quarters under escort of gendarmes.
- Second, they may carry on their journey movable property, but they may not sell lands or other significant property "because their exile is only temporary."

- Third, they are promised safe-conduct.
- Fourth, they will not be molested on their journey.
- Fifth, any attempt to evade or resist the order is prohibited.

This précis is based on a digest of the proclamation smuggled out of Turkey by an American woman, Eleanor Franklin Egan, and published in the *Saturday Evening Post,* February 5, 1916.[5] (The genocide proceeded under a blanket of censorship.) The stated rules, needless to say, were abominably violated, in fact were a travesty of the actual conduct of the deportation. In the Ottoman Empire the gap between what was decreed and what was done could never be underestimated, as most Armenians understood. The journeys the Armenians—mostly women and children—were sent upon coursed into mountains and deserts where there was neither food nor shelter nor safe-conduct of any degree. The journeys were meant to end in the Armenians' death individually and collectively. To be sure, favored women and children might elude the decree, with its terrible fate, by submission to their Muslim captors. For men escape was much more difficult, as it required change of name, of language, circumcision, and adoption of Islam.

Johannes Lepsius, the German observer, made his own record of the deportations. It began with Erzroom on May 15 and proceeded through the cities of the Anatolian tableland, thence to Cilicia.[6] A prosperous market city and military stronghold, in the province of the same name, Erzroom counted 20,000 Armenians. In the peasant villages of the sprawling plain were 45,000. First the villagers were rounded up and sent off, then the townspeople. They were allowed several days to dispose of their property. Some 1,400 bales of goods were deposited in the care of American missionaries. Well-to-do families, it was said, set off with five or more oxcarts loaded with household goods. By the end of the year fewer than one hundred Armenians were left in Erzroom and the city had fallen into decay.[7]

At Trebizond, beautifully situated in the mountains above the Black Sea, the proclamation had been posted on June 26, and four days later the streets were guarded by gendarmes with fixed bayonets as the work of driving the Armenians from their homes began. Some, it was said, were herded into boats and drowned at sea. Most were gathered into convoys numbering about two thousand. "By the 6th of July," according to an eyewitness, "all the Armenian houses in Trebizond, about 1,000, had been emptied of their inhabitants and the people sent off." Local Turks, who had been enjoying an Armenian fire sale, quickly moved in.[8] The Italian consul was traumatized by these events. "I no longer slept or ate; I was given over to nerves and nausea, so terrible was the torment of having to look on at the execution of these defenseless, innocent victims." The city seemed in a state of siege:

> The passing of the gangs of Armenian exiles beneath the windows and before the door of the Consulate . . . the lamentations, tears, the abandonments, the imprecations, the many suicides, the instantaneous deaths from sheer terror, the sudden unhinging of men's reason, the conflagrations, the shooting of victims in the city, the ruthless searches through the houses and in the countryside; the hundreds of corpses found every day along the exile road; the young women converted by force to Islam or exiled like the rest; the children torn away from their families or from Christian schools, and handed over by force to Moslem families, or else packed by hundreds on board ship in nothing but their shirts, and then capsized and drowned in the Black Sea and the River Deyirmen Deré—these are my last ineffable memories of Trebizond.

When the consul left the city on July 23, not a hundred of the 14,000 Armenians who had formerly lived there remained.[9]

Harpoot, or Kharpert, the principal city in the vilayet of Mamouret-ul-Aziz, is a particularly revealing case for the study of the genocide. Rising above the central plain and ringed by mountains with elevations of upwards of 3,000 feet, as described by an English traveler in 1898, Harpoot was surrounded by a hundred or more villages.

> The vine flourishes and is cultivated at this moderate eleva-
> tion; and the dwellings are for the most part constructed of
> mud and brick with two storeys, in striking contrast to the
> unhealthy underground burrows in which the peasantry
> cheat the rigor of an Armenian winter over the great portion
> of the tableland. Pear and plum trees grace the outskirts of
> the settlement, and mulberry grows in such profusion that
> the silk crop is often of considerable value.[10]

Armenians were preponderant in the countryside, while in the city they were a minority of the 30,000 inhabitants. There was a missionary station, in which the indefatigable Riggs family were conspicuous; and also a college named for the river Euphrates, which flowed through the province. Two eyewitnesses wrote extraordinarily full and perceptive reports on the genocide in Harpoot. One was Dr. Henry H. Riggs, the Congregational minister who had previously presided over the college. His report was written after he returned to the United States, and it later formed the basis of a memoir, *Days of Tragedy in Armenia*, published in 1997. The other was Leslie A. Davis, American consul at Harpoot from 1914 to 1917. His account was undertaken at the request of the State Department upon his return home. A New York lawyer who had seen service in Batum, Davis was thirty-nine years of age when he occupied the handsome consulate in Harpoot. A diligent researcher, Susan K. Blair, rescued the report from the archives in 1989, and it was published under the title *The Slaughterhouse Province*. Davis himself had thought to bestow this name on the vilayet. While there are minor discrepancies in the two accounts, they complement, complete, and reinforce each other.

Armenian citizens in Harpoot being led away under armed guard, May 1915

After the Sublime Porte abrogated the capitulations in 1914, the *vali* (governor) of the province ordered Euphrates College to close its doors, and Riggs waited apprehensively for the sequel to unfold. Yet at this time he thought the feelings between Turks and Armenians were good. The air was free of racial animosity and religious fanaticism. When the lightning struck, it clearly was not from the people. The infamous deportation edict was posted on June 26. "This announcement was made by the town crier, Mahmoud Chavonosh," Davis wrote, "who went around the streets, accompanied by a small boy beating a drum, and called out the terrible proclamation in a stentorian voice."[11] Suddenly the men, including the most prominent, were disarmed, arrested, imprisoned, bastinadoed, terrorized, and murdered. On one occasion, Riggs observed, eight hundred men were taken from prison, bound in groups of four, marched ten miles into the mountains, seated on the crest of a ridge, and forthwith attacked by the guards with rifles and bayonets, "a butchery that the imagination refuses to picture." One of the victims escaped to tell of the horror.[12]

Upon hearing the deportation proclamation, Armenians scrambled to sell or arrange for the safekeeping of their property. The government appointed a Committee for Abandoned Goods whose ostensible purpose was to secure the money and goods of deported Armenians, but little confidence was placed in this promise, and indeed, it proved hollow. Davis thought the way the committee later wound up its affairs a good illustration of Turkish methods. "After it [the committee] had gotten possession of hundreds of thousands of dollars, it conveniently lost its books and explained that, as all the money received had been used up for expenses and there were no funds on hand, there was no necessity anyway of rendering any account!" Equally pertinent was the vali's comment to Riggs: "'Every person sent into exile is considered by the government as dead.'" Riggs added, "The supposition was fairly near the truth." Many Armenians sought the safety of the consulate for their valuables. Davis's safe was filled with jewelry and gold. Riggs, too, found himself in the bank business. "I was simply deluged with money," he wrote, much of it gold. Wherever possible, he remitted the money to the United States. He also made deposits in the Ottoman Bank. The government subsequently appropriated them.[13] In all the dealings involving abandoned property, pillage, thievery, and fraud were omnipresent.

The Armenians being the storekeepers, the traders and merchants, the doctors, lawyers, and artisans, their forcible exile offered a grand opportunity for plunder and enrichment by their oppressors. J. B. Jackson, Davis's counterpart in Aleppo, concluded, "It is a gigantic plundering scheme as well as a final blow to extinguish the race."[14] This was the avaricious side of the genocide. "Our noble Vali," Riggs commented, "after the deportation, immediately moved into the most magnificent mansion in the town." The hitch in this familiar story of covetousness and greed was that the Turks were wholly unprepared to assume the work of the society earlier performed by the Armenians. "By one stroke the country was to be set back a century," Davis wrote. Nor was this vacuum limited to trades and professions. "In the Harput region most of the agriculture also was carried on by Armenians. . . . It was literally a case of killing the goose that laid the golden egg, for there would be no one left to till the soil."[15]

The first exodus from Harpoot occurred on July 1. The night before gendarmes had gone among the Armenian homes chalking on each door "Deportation" or "Postponement." (Protestants and Catholics were temporarily exempted, for instance.) Three thousand women and children made up the first convoy, accompanied by donkeys and oxen and carts or wagons loaded with possessions.[16] They proceeded on foot under guard of the hated gendarmes, who in the absence of able-bodied young men, taken into the army, were the dregs of the prison population. Riggs remarked upon "the relentless efficiency" of the whole operation; in truth, however, it had none of the bureaucratic efficiency later achieved by the Germans in the Holocaust. It would take a volume to describe the brutalities and sufferings of the long and arduous march southward. By September, according to Davis, three-fourths of the Armenians of "the slaughterhouse province" had been deported. They went without resistance and with what Riggs called "Christian courage." As one van pulled out, a woman looked back, waved, and called cheerfully, "Good-bye! We are going to heaven! Meet us there."[17] A memorandum sent to the American Committee for Armenian and Syrian Relief detailed the fate of the first caravan from Harpoot. It had been decimated by unruly gendarmes, by Kurdish brigands, by typhus and dysentery, above all by starvation. On the seventieth day, having traveled a thousand miles, the survivors, numbering thirty-five women and children, reached the southern terminus, Aleppo.[18] (The general estimate was that 20 percent of

Armenian refugees on the march through Alexandropol

the deported reached their destination.) Those who ended up in the "resettlement zone" of the lower Euphrates were to be pitied rather than congratulated. An American businessman who happened to be in Der-el-Zor wrote to Consul Jackson of the horrible tableaux: "As on the gates of 'Hell' of Dante, the following should be written at the entrance to these accursed encampments: 'You who enter, leave all hope.'"[19]

Consul Davis, in Harpoot, also had occasion to think of Dante's *Inferno* that summer. A year earlier he, with other townspeople, had escaped the oppressive heat of the city at nearby Lake Goeljuk. In 1915, however, this spot, like other open spaces, had become a killing ground of the wretched Armenian exiles. Making a tour around the lake, Davis and his companion repeatedly stumbled on the refuse of the genocide: an arm here, a head there, a dead infant. "We estimated in the course of our ride around the lake, and actually within the space of twenty-four hours, we had seen the remains of not less than ten thousand Armenians." Few locations could be better suited to the Turks' fiendish purposes, he went on. "Thousands and thousands of Armenians, mostly innocent and helpless women and children, were butchered on its shore and barbarously mutilated." And none to sound an alarm! Hard as it was to believe such things possible, Davis was reminded of Lord Bryce's comment: "Things which we find scarcely credible excite little surprise in Turkey."[20]

Davis continued in his post until May 16, 1917, when he returned to the United States, now at war with Germany. Reverend Riggs returned at the same time. Neither found much to occupy his time after the expulsion of the Armenians. The college was closed; the churches had lost their congregations; most of the missionary families had gone home. A lone Danish missionary, Maria Jacobsen, remained. People asked Riggs what, if anything, was left of the American missionary effort of three-quarters of a century. It was impossible to think that one's life had been wasted. There was a saving vestige, Riggs said: "the calm triumphant faith that only the indwelling power of Christ could sustain in that dark hour."[21] Both Davis and Riggs found themselves engaged in a kind of low-grade relief work. After the abrogation of capitulations, even though the United States declined to recognize it, the consul had little else to do. He sought to save the lives of Armenian Americans who happened to be visiting the homeland in 1915; and he invested considerable effort in tracing the lives and property of Armenians at the behest of their American relations. As he did so, Davis grew more and more despondent over the case of the Armenians. He wrote to Ambassador Morgenthau just before his departure:

> One of the disappointments in the present terrible situation and one of the saddest commentaries on American missionary work among the Armenians is their lack of religion and moral principles and the general baseness of the race. During all that has happened the past year I have not heard of a single act of heroism or of self-sacrifice and the nobler acts, if any, have been very few.[22]

This criticism was harsh, and it must be said unfair. It tended to shift the moral burden of the genocide to the victims. Davis surely knew of the resistance at Van, and he should have known of the heroism at Urfa and Musa Dagh, still to be recounted.

Perhaps nowhere was the carnage worse than in Cilicia. For not only were its own Armenian inhabitants massacred, but the ragged convoys from the north converged there. "Aleppo," it was said, "served as the switchyard for the deportations." It was bursting at the seams. American relief workers were among the first to extend a helping hand. Survivors were sent from there to the death camps of Der-el-Zor and thereabouts in the deserts of Mesopotamia. In March 1916 a Turkish official filed an interim report with the authorities in the capital: "Thirty-five thousand dead in the area of El Bab and Meskin; ten thousand in Aleppo . . . twenty thousand near Dibse, Abu-Herrera, Quaragol, Hannan; thirty-five thousand at Ras-el-Ain; a total of a hundred thousand victims. And then there are the Armenian refugees from Damascus, and especially Deir es Zor, at least two hundred thousand." An Armenian survivor gasped before the scene from hell: "Corpses! Corpses! Murdered! Mutilated! Corpses of Armenian men, women, and children!"[23]

"The Cilician Armenians were mainly shepherds and husbandmen," Lord Bryce wrote, "but they were also one of the most civilized and progressive sections of the Armenian race." The adoption of modern ideas and techniques that in Bryce's eyes made them "most civilized," of course, made them all the more obnoxious to the Ottoman rulers. Along the Gulf of Alexandretta, in the vilayet of Aleppo, lay the six villages of Musa Dagh (Mount Moses), with the mountain rising above them. To one of the villages, Yoghanalouk, the Reverend Dikran Andressian, a native, had been ordered to return with his wife from his pulpit in the Armenian Protestant Church of Zeitun, where the deportation had already begun. "My heart was torn between the desire to share banishment with some fragment of my congregation and the desire to take my wife to a place of comparative safety in my father's home." Here, in the historic valley of Antioch, in a village scented by the bloom of fruit and mulberry trees, he wrote, "the broad rough back of Musa Dagh . . . rises up eastward behind us. Every gorge and crag of our beloved mountain is known to our boys and men." Eight days after the pastor's return, the order of banishment reached the villages. At a mass meeting, the people sat up all night debating what to do. Resistance, where it had been tried, had been crushed. Another Armenian pastor spoke up in opposition. But Andressian and a small army of villagers decided to resist. Their plan was to withdraw immediately to the heights of Musa Dagh. With them they took supplies of food, sheep and goats, and whatever firearms came to hand. The first day on the mountain they dug defensive trenches, and in a great meeting that evening they elected a committee of defense. The Congregational method of choice by secret ballot was followed meticulously, according to Andressian. "Our people have become very attached to these democratic methods taught by the missionaries."[24]

On the eighth day, a Turkish force scaled the mountain from the sea and attacked the settlement. It was driven back. "But the Turks were gathering force for a massed attack. They had sent word through many Moslem villages, calling the people to arms." When the second assault came, the Armenians were at first overwhelmed, but then by an ingenious encircling maneuver confounded the invaders and forced their retreat after inflicting heavy losses. Next the Turks mounted an attack on the landward side, laying siege with the intention of starving out the mountain defenders. Now desperate measures became necessary. A runner was sent eighty-five miles to Aleppo to appeal to the American consul for help. There was no response. (Actually, the runner reached Aleppo and delivered his message to Consul Jackson, but it proved unavailing.) Next a swimmer was dispatched to search for a passing warship in the gulf. This effort, too, failed. On the fortieth day, three swimmers went off carrying an appeal, and two immense flags emblazoning a red cross with the inscription, in English, "CHRISTIANS IN DISTRESS: RESCUE," was flown from tall saplings on the mountain summit. Finally, on a Sunday morning, the fifty-third day, while Andressian was preparing his sermon, news came that a warship in the harbor had answered the distress call. It was the French cruiser *Guichen*, which was then joined by the flagship *Ste Jeanne d'Arc*. Four French and one British cruisers eventually took aboard some four thousand refugees—men, women, and children—and discharged them at Port Said, in Egypt, where they came under the care of the newly formed Armenian Red Cross. It was, as Lord Bryce remarked in the fat Foreign Office blue book *The Treatment of the Armenians,* in 1916, "the only story in this volume with a happy ending."[25] The heroic resistance later formed the historical basis of Franz Werfel's great novel, *The Forty Days of Musa Dagh.*

In the city of Urfa (or Ourfa), northeast of Aleppo, valiant Armenians also took the path of resistance, but met with tragic defeat. An eyewitness wrote, "They entrenched themselves strongly in their quarter, built barricades, made subterranean passages from one part of the quarter to another, and generally took every measure possible to defend themselves against attack." A Turkish army of 6,000 was thrown against them. Intermittent battle raged through the month of October, until the enemy broke through the barricades. One of the Armenian survivors, Ephraim K. Jernagian, then twenty-five, would later write: "To avoid falling into the hands of the Turks, some shot their wives, children, and themselves. Some piled their furniture in one room and, lighting a fire to the heap, threw themselves as a family into the flames. Others threw themselves into wells. Some hid in underground passages but were often found and slain." Several of the fighters taken captive were hanged in the city square. Women and children were herded into the courtyard of the Apostolic church. (One of the Armenian churches, it may be recalled, had been burned with its occupants in the siege of 1895.) An Islamic mullah, wielding a sword, is said to have addressed them: "Listen, you *giavoors* [infidels]. Last night in my dreams I saw the prophet Mohammed. He ordered me to sacrifice 100 Armenian male children under one year of age in your sanctuary at the altar." Soldiers delivered the tiny children, it was said, and they were decapitated one by one at the altar.[26] The genocide produced atrocities of all kinds; however, manifestations of religious fanaticism of this degree were unusual.

The American press had been reacting to the Armenian catastrophe since the conflict at Van in the spring of 1915. Turkish censorship was effective only to a point. The return to the United States of Dr. Clarence Ussher and Ernest Yarrow, both formerly attached to the now defunct missionary station at Van, coincided with the formation of the American Committee for Armenian and Syrian Relief, prompted by Ambassador Morgenthau's urgent summons. The story of Musa Dagh in the fall was a fillip to the organization's $5 million campaign. A share of the receipts of the Harvard-Yale football game that fall went to Armenian relief, and the revivalist Billy Sunday filled the Detroit Tabernacle with the watchword: "A dollar a week will sustain ten people a week in Asia Minor."[27] Weekly magazines such as the *Independent* and *Outlook* ran stories on the Armenian atrocities. An American foreign correspondent, Herbert Adams Gibbons, well informed on the Near East, wrote a seventy-one-page tract for popular consumption, *The Blackest Page of Modern History.*

No one could reliably estimate the Armenian death toll. Bryce, at the time his great collection of documents went to press in July 1916, thought it ranged between 800,000 and one million. William W. Rockwell, a professor at Union Theological Seminary and associated in humanitarian relief, generally concurred, though he admonished, "In the desert vultures were the only coroners." In order to reduce the abstract number to something the mind could grasp, Rockwell asked readers to think of the huge Preparedness Day parade in New York in May, when it took 125,000 marchers, twenty abreast, thirteen hours to pass. "If the ghosts of the Christian civilians who have perished miserably since the commencement of the great holocaust should march down Fifth Avenue twenty abreast there might be a million of them, and they would take four days and eight hours to pass the great reviewing stand."[28] Bryce's 684-page tome, *Treatment of the Armenians*, was abridged in a three-page spread in the *New York Times* on October 8, 1916, coincident with the launching of the Armenian Relief campaign.

Initially, in some quarters, it was suspected that the British were pricking American altruistic impulses in order to provoke the country's entrance into the war. Bryce himself, of course, was a much respected figure in the United States. He could not be dismissed as a war propagandist. The other side of the coin was the vision of Germany as the hidden hand behind the genocide. All the more reason

Victims

Refugee camp in the desert

to declare war on Germany. Like Pilate, Germany had washed its hands of the killing. Dr. Martin Niepage, a German eyewitness in Aleppo, published in London, then in the United States, a one-penny pamphlet, *The Horrors of Aleppo.* "'Ta'alim el aleman' ('the teaching of the Germans') is the simple Turk's explanation to everyone who asks him about the origination of these measures." Others added that the Armenians stood in the way of Germany's *Drang nach Osten*—its imperious drive to Baghdad and beyond. Arnold Toynbee, who was Bryce's collaborator on the blue book, would later argue that even if the massacres could be used as war propaganda, the historical evidence of the genocide would not therefore be invalidated. And the historical evidence was so overwhelming and so persuasive that it was simply recalcitrant to label it propaganda.[29]

In the opinion of an observant Armenian, Aram Andonian, "the most terrible crimes and the greatest massacres took place after 1916." There are several ways in which this might be shown to be true; but Andonian referred to the toll of slaughter among the exiles in Mesopotamia. An Armenian intellectual living in Constantinople in 1915, Andonian had been arrested and exiled to Diarbekir, a provincial capital on the Tigris River, which he called an infamous place. He escaped and made acquaintance with Naim Bey, the chief secretary of the Deportations Committee at Aleppo, who had earlier gone on special assignment to the lower Euphrates to clear the glut of the dead and dying there. Naim Bey was a turncoat. The Young Turk rulers, the Ittihad (CUP), sought to destroy written evidence of the crimes; but Naim Bey had hidden away whatever he could, together with firsthand evidence from surviving victims. He had made himself, as Andonian said, "a voice of conscience." According to Naim Bey, there were huge massacres after 1916: at Ras-ul-Ain, the present terminus of the Baghdad Railroad, where 70,000 were killed; at Intilli, among the 50,000 forced to labor on a tunnel of the railroad; and at the aforementioned Der-el-Zor, where 200,000 Armenians were slaughtered. Most of these victims had survived the deportation. Naim Bey estimated that 10 to 25 percent, varying from one caravan to another, arrived at their destination, and so had to be killed in other ways. He called the idea that the Armenians met death from "natural causes" a farce. Naim Bey showed Andonian a copy of an order, probably originating with Talaat, challenging deportation officials to put aside all feelings of pity and "try with all your might to obliterate the very name 'Armenia' from Turkey." When an official at Aleppo, crowded with the refuse of the deportations, called attention to the need for orphanages, Talaat replied, "There is no need for an orphanage. . . . Send them [the children] away to the desert." He underscored the importance, as a safeguard, of erasing the very memory of the genocide. Little children, too young to remember, might be spared. One order read: "All Armenians in the country who are Ottoman subjects, from five years of age upwards, are to be taken out of the towns and slaughtered." Other orders shown to Andonian pertained to confiscation of property—the spoils of the genocide.[30]

One of the pervasive Turkish exculpations for the genocide was that it had been provoked by the Armenians. The idea, as formulated by one analyst, was "that the potential victim is artfully pushed into acts of desperation by the political perpetrator in order to create a temporary expedient for unleashing the assault."[31] Victim and assassin thus change places. The Turkish consul general in New York, responding to the report of the American Committee on the Armenian Atrocities, declared: "However much to be deplored may be these harrowing events, in the last analysis we can but say the Armenians have only themselves to blame."[32] Had not they been plotting revolution? Had not they taken up arms against the empire? And there were other provocations. A vali justified the attack on the Armenians in this way: "They had grown in wealth and numbers until they had become a menace to the ruling Turkish race; extermination was the only remedy."[33] This was a socially specific explanation arising from the fear of domination by the subject people. As for charges of revolution and treason, scarcely one Armenian in a hundred, as Gibbons observed, had any connection with these offenses. Most charges of treason and disloyalty ran against Armenians in the Caucasus, who, as a rule, were Russian subjects.

Socially, the worm of envy was at work among the Turks. Many of them had enjoyed good relationships with the Armenians. Religion had not been an inflammatory issue. Toleration was the rule within the multinational Ottoman Empire and the foundation of the distribution of power to millets, which were separate religious communities, the Armenians being one, possessed of substantial autonomy. Besides, most of the Muslims in the empire were not Turks but Arabs, who did not entertain the same enmity toward the Armenian Christian minority. Moreover, the Young Turks—at least those in power in Constantinople—openly scoffed at religion. Some were closet atheists. In Toynbee's considered opinion, "There was no Moslem passion against the Armenian Christians. All was done by the will of the Government, and done not from any religious fanaticism but simply because they wished, for reasons purely political, to get rid of a non-Moslem element that might not always submit to oppression."[34] The ideological division between Turk and Armenian was real and important, however. Westernization among the educated Armenians placed them at odds with the xenophobic Young Turks. One analyst has argued that the Armenian Christians were in danger of losing their status as a legitimate millet within the empire and becoming, instead, a rival nationality. This development could only add to friction between the two groups.[35]

And how did the victims understand or explain the great crime to themselves? Only through the power of their religious faith. God had not betrayed the Armenians. He had, miraculously, raised up and sustained their nation for many centuries. One of the faithful wrote on the eve of his exile:

> From this we realize that God can and has shut the mouths of lions for many years. May God restrain them! I am afraid they may kill some of us, cast some of us into cruel starvation and send the rest out of the country. . . . But be sure, by God's special help, I will do my best to encourage others to die manly. I will also look for God's help for myself to die as a Christian. . . . May God forgive this nation all their sins. May the Armenians teach Jesus' life by their death, which they could not teach by their life or have failed in showing forth.[36]

The last chapter of the Armenian genocide had yet to be written when the United States declared war on Germany in April 1917, and was precipitated by the meteoric rise of Turkish nationalism behind an army commanded by Mustafa Kemal as the war drew to a close. And if we are to understand that development, together with its bearing on the Armenian Question, the events must be set in appropriate context. The United States' declaration of war pointedly did not extend to Turkey. Although diplomatic relations between the two countries had earlier been severed by Turkey's choice, the United States maintained a posture of neutrality toward that country, a staunch ally of the German Reich. When the war ended and the belligerents turned their attention to making peace, there would be a good deal of second-guessing of President Wilson's decision to remain neutral toward Turkey. The former president Theodore Roosevelt, a zealot for the Armenians, thought it craven and pusillanimous. In this decision Wilson appears to have been motivated mainly by a desire to protect American missionary and educational interests in Turkey and to maintain leverage with the Sublime Porte in the great work of humanitarian relief that arose to stem the backwash of the genocide.

3 | Near East Relief in War and Peace

THE MEN WHO MET in New York City on September 16, 1915, in answer to Ambassador Henry Morgenthau's urgent call for humanitarian relief in the Near East, were an impressive group, one that bore the stamp of the half-century Protestant missionary and educational movement in that part of the world. The two conveners, James Levi Barton and Cleveland H. Dodge, respectively of Boston and New York, were veterans in this endeavor. Barton, sixty years old, was born in Vermont and went to college at Middlebury; after graduation he attended Hartford Theological Seminary and became an ordained Congregational minister in 1885. That same year he went out as a missionary to Harpoot in Turkey. Later he became president of Euphrates College, and thereafter was foreign secretary of the American Board of Commissioners of Foreign Missions, in Constantinople. The Dodge family had been at work in the missionary field for three generations. Attending Princeton, the young Cleveland Dodge met Woodrow Wilson in 1875, and the classmates became lifelong friends. Dodge pursued an industrial career and was well known as a copper baron and philanthropist. Barton was elected chairman of the organization formed on this auspicious occasion, and Dodge, who offered his office for the meeting, after a brief interval became its treasurer. They were heart and soul of the American Committee for Armenian and Syrian Relief, which evolved into Near East Relief (NER) upon its incorporation by act of Congress in 1919.[1]

Morgenthau, crowned with laurels of glory for his exposure of the genocide, rapidly became the leading spokesman for Near East Relief. With the permission of the State Department he consulted with Barton and his friends on the American Board in Boston, and with a nod from President Wilson embarked on a two-week speaking tour that took him from Philadelphia to St. Louis and Chicago and was capped with a Sunday-evening address at Carnegie Hall in New York. The ambassador's story was many Americans' introduction to the strange land they were asked to aid and succor. Few had ever encountered an Armenian or could locate the country the Armenians inhabited on a map. Approximately 100,000 Armenians lived in the United States, of whom perhaps 30 percent were naturalized citizens.[2] They were concentrated in small colonies mainly in the northeastern states, nowhere in sufficient numbers to command much interest, let alone political influence. Upon his return from the tour, Morgenthau submitted his resignation as ambassador to Turkey, and the president accepted it on May 23, 1916.[3] His successor, Abram L. Elkus, was named without delay, though the Ottoman government was slow to signify its acceptance.

The work of Barton and his organization began, first, with building a staff at home and overseas. Its size fluctuated, of course, peaking in the years after the war, but it finally numbered two to three thousand people. Several of the top officials served without compensation; and NER, as a strictly private organization, depended on the volunteer spirit of its workers, just as the United States Peace Corps does today. In time committees in every state plus Alaska and Hawaii became indispensable auxiliaries. Second, the organization undertook to build a following among the American people, and from them to raise money and in-kind support for humanitarian relief abroad. This effort required a campaign of public education, utilizing the whole battery of public relations and fund-raising skills. It required, bluntly, propaganda in the service of a good cause. In the book he later wrote, *Story of Near East Relief,* Barton emphasized that the organization was wholly nonpolitical, and he cited as an example the question of declaring war on Turkey in 1917, on which, while internal opinion was divided, NER took no public position.[4] In matters touching its own interests internationally as well, NER steered clear of political entanglements. Political neutrality was believed to be necessary to maintain the humanitarian character of the movement. An essential ally in its mobilization of American opinion was the press, and NER was fortunate in the support it received. As Barton acknowledged, "the press of the entire country has been sympathetic, helpful and liberal to the last degree."[5] No newspaper was more supportive or more thoughtful in its commentary than the *New York Times,* one of whose editors, John H. Finley, was also a sometime member of NER's board of trustees. The weekly *Literary Digest* should also be singled out for its aid and assistance to the organization's mission.

That mission was the delivery of direct relief to victims of Turkish atrocities committed mainly but not exclusively against the Armenians in the Near East. Getting food, medicine, clothing, and necessary equipment and supplies to the people in need was surrounded by difficulty during the years of war. In the beginning relief had been channeled through Morgenthau at Constantinople. A glitch developed after he left, but before long the Ottoman government signaled its receptivity to American humanitarian aid administered under the direction of NER's so-called Constantinople Committee. Its chairman was Caleb Gates, president of Robert College. Its treasurer was William W. Peet, resident secretary of the American Board of Commissioners for Foreign Missions. "Our relief work is assuming proportions that we could not have comprehended a few months ago," Peet wrote in 1916. He estimated that upwards of 500,000 refugees, mostly women and children, and mostly Armenians, were receiving relief from the committee.[6] There was no essential change during the next two years, in part because the United States remained neutral toward Turkey. Morgenthau even prevailed upon the president to send a naval vessel, the U.S.S. *Collier,* loaded with emergency supplies, upon the promise of the Turkish government that it would be received. From the speaker's platform he was able to assure ordinary American citizens that if they dug into their pocket for a dollar it would find a secure channel to the needy in Turkey. Moreover, because Dodge quietly covered the organization's campaign and administrative expenses, it could advertise that "100 cents of every dollar goes for relief." After the rupture of diplomatic relations in 1917, Elkus wrote in the *Times,* "The American Committee for Armenian and Syrian Relief is known throughout the length and breadth of Turkey, and is the hope of despairing and hungry people of many faiths, and, in many cases, the only hope." As Barton attested, the Sublime Porte remained receptive after American relief workers were made attachés of the Swedish legation, charged with the care of American interests.[7]

The nexus between Near East Relief and the foreign missionary movement of the Congregational Church is manifest in the presence of Barton and Peet at the helm, one at Congregational House on Boston's Beacon Hill, the other at Bible House in Constantinople. For both men it must have been difficult at times to separate the work of one hand from the other, the work of the missionary from the humanitarian. The most scrupulous care could not prevent the intermingling of accounts, financial and otherwise. The American Board and NER shared facilities and personnel and they served the same Armenian clientele. This overlap, while not planned, developed with unfolding events. By the time Lorin A. Shephard, for instance, took up his duties as a missionary at Aintab in August 1919, he would observe, "The institutions of the station have been largely given over to the work of ACRNE [American

Committee for Relief in the Near East]. School buildings are being used for orphanage purposes. The hospital is being run as an ACRNE hospital." Shephard split his time between missionary and relief work and thought the coordination of the two a problem.[8]

Wartime relief followed the marching of armies from the Caucasus to the Sinai. The tsar's armies returned to the Caucasus in 1916, forcing the Turks to withdraw and reclaiming Armenian lands from Trebizond to Lake Van, alas now largely bereft of Armenians. In February Frederick W. MacCallum took leave of his missionary post in Marash to lead a relief expedition from London through the Baltic to Petrograd, then south to Erivan and Lake Sevan. Van, of course, was in ruins. MacCallum and his three associates brought food and clothing and attempted to resupply refugee farmers, who numbered in tens of thousands. The committee, aided by the American consul in Tiflis (now Tbilisi), was, at the minimum, a boost to morale. MacCallum, who upon his return worked in the New York office of Near East Relief, wrote to Barton of the dark underside of the experience.

> I heard a great many stories of individual sufferings—men flayed alive, hacked to pieces with axes, starved to death, buried alive, burned to death, starved to death in holes of indescribable filth, of women outraged in the most cruel and disgusting manner, pregnant women ripped open, breasts cut off, delicate, refined young women compelled to travel day after day perfectly naked, innumerable cases of women being forced into Moslem harems; of children also tortured and killed in the most brutal manner. But all I have seen myself are some of the effects of this treatment, scars, sickness, insanity, fright, desperation, hatred, desire for revenge on the Turks, etc.[9]

MacCallum's trajectory from missionary work abroad to relief work at home was not unusual. Most of the schools and colleges had closed, either because of declining enrollments or because the facilities were commandeered by the Turkish army. This was especially the case after the rupture of diplomatic relations in the spring of 1917. Hospitals, too, were appropriated. The only college to remain open throughout the war was Smyrna International College, located in the mountains called Paradise. Enrollment plummeted from 400 to 100 students, many of them Muslim. The Muslim students forced the question, sometimes discussed by the missionaries, of evangelization among the Turks. The president, Dr. Alexander MacLachlan, widely respected, was told by Turkish officials he must excuse Muslim students from compulsory chapel services. To this mandate he replied that everyone must attend chapel or leave the college. The students held an "indignation meeting" and enlisted the aid of Professor Ralph Harlow, who was also head of the YMCA, but without success. A standoff ensued.

George E. White, president of Anatolia College, in Marsovan, returned home to work for NER in Minnesota. "I am getting into relief work as the first interest," he was soon writing. "Always and everywhere I am a missionary, and even if I am disposed to drop the College for a time it would not drop me, but bread is the great need among 'our people' in Turkey now."[10] White, with other returnees, often spoke in public for NER. Edith Cold, supervisor of Christian schools in Hadjin, had witnessed the trek of exiles in Cilicia. "Our horizon has so greatly changed we hardly recognize ourselves," she wrote in 1915, and she added significantly that the missionaries had all taken to reading the poet Henry Wadsworth Longfellow's *Evangeline,* about the exile of the Acadians from Nova Scotia. "So vivid are the events and so often do we read it that we know it by heart."[11] Miss Cold later returned to her home in Ann Arbor, Michigan. Secretary Peet, on June 17, 1917, followed Ambassador Elkus to Switzerland, setting up first in Berne, then in Geneva, as liaison between the United States and the Near East, having already prepared a "Memorandum Concerning Relief Work in the Turkish Empire" for the guidance of the State Department. In time he, too, returned to the United States.

Thousands of desperate refugees, many of them Armenian, converged on Jerusalem in 1918 after its capture by General Allenby of Britain's Egyptian Expeditionary Force. Katherine Fisher, a relief worker, reported to NER, "They have been wandering for three years and have scarcely a rag to cover them."[12] She went on to describe the effort to feed and shelter and clothe the refugees. The Red Cross was first on the ground in Palestine because it was a war zone in 1918. John H. Finley, an educator on leave from his post on the New York State Board of Regents, was named Red Cross high commissioner for Palestine. Something of a poet, Finley later wrote a book, *A Pilgrim in Palestine,* about his experience there. A cordial friend of Near East Relief, he celebrated Bible precepts of Bible lands and composed "A New Harmony of the Gospels," which juxtaposed descriptions of destitute Armenians with the New Testament Gospel. In March 1919, as the Red Cross abandoned the field, NER assumed full responsibility for relief under the amicable terms of "the treaty of Konia," as it was named, negotiated between Finley and Barton. Upon his return to the United States, Finley became a valuable member of NER's board of directors. Sometime later, as lead editor of the *New York Times,* he lent his pen to the increasingly desperate cause of the Armenian nation.[13]

The British advance in Mesopotamia freed untold numbers of ragged survivors from Turkish captivity. A cable datelined Baghdad to NER's New York office read: "Hundreds of emaciated refugees arriving daily. Funds needed." In Teheran, a city of about 350,000, two-thirds of the people were starving. A relief worker wrote, "We have divided the city into nine districts, in each of which there is a center from which rice and money are given out each Friday to 20,000 people."[14] As the Russian army withdrew from the Caucasian front in the wake of the Treaty of Brest-Litovsk, the Turks moved in and resumed the practice of slaughtering Armenians.

Dispatches from Tiflis advised that some 350,000 people in that area required a minimum allowance of $3 a month to survive. Suddenly the specter of untold numbers of orphaned children loomed large. NER, together with the American Board, had sent out a small corps of nurses to take up relief work among the orphans in 1917. In October of that year, President Wilson issued an "Appeal to the American People" on behalf of the orphans. And Rabbi Stephen Wise, in an address at New York's Hippodrome, solemnly warned, "If the 100,000 orphans alive in Armenia today are allowed to starve, the Armenian race will be destroyed." The task of saving the lives of refugees exacted a grim toll on the aid workers. In the year ending September 1918, NER reported in its *News Bulletin,* "eighteen workers in the field had lost their lives."[15]

By January 1, 1918, Near East Relief had raised almost $7 million. That sum was paltry in light of the need perceived a year later. Some of the money came from munificent philanthropies such as the Rockefeller Foundation, some of it came from the Red Cross, but most of it came from the pennies of schoolchildren and the dollars of hardworking Americans. Public relations appeals stereotyped "the Terrible Turk" and sentimentalized the Armenians. They were massacred, starved, the women ravished, the children orphaned. They were Christians, and Christian righteousness pervaded appeals on their behalf. Churches and church leaders, through preaching and fast days and neighborly calling, were prominent in the fund-raising effort. Yet the appeal was also imbued with the pride and patriotism of the American people, as if the nation, or a substantial portion thereof, had adopted Armenia as an orphan people worthy of its embrace. Katherine Lee Bates, the Wellesley poet and author of "America the Beautiful," seemed to add the "spacious skies" of that far-off country to those of her own.

> Armenia! The name is like a sword
>   In every Christian heart. O martyr nation,

Eldest of all the daughters of the Word,
>Exceeding all in bitter tribulation!

Armenia! The name is like a cry
>Of agony that shrills around the sphere.
Bread, bread before her last starved children die
>And tell to Christ how cold our hearts are here.

Armenia! A figure on a cross,
>Pale, wasted, bleeding, with imploring eyes!
Except we save her, darkness lies across
>All Christendom, shamed in her sacrifice.[16]

NER's most ambitious public relations venture was the result less of design than of fortuitous circumstances. This was the motion picture *Ravished Armenia*. It purported to be the true story of an Armenian girl, Aurora Mardiganian, who had survived the deportation; even more miraculously, she voyaged to America in 1918 in search of two missing brothers and was met at Ellis Island by an Armenian American couple. Her pathetic story, picked up in the press, attracted the interest of Nora Waln, publicity secretary of NER, and of Harvey Gates, a screenwriter. He signed Aurora, then seventeen and very pretty, to star in a motion picture for $15 a month, and jointly with his wife became her legal guardian, then whisked her off to Los Angeles. The rights to Aurora's story were acquired by a veteran producer, William N. Selig. The film was shot at Mount Baldy, behind Santa Barbara, the stand-in for Ararat. The credits for the film read "Produced for the American Committee for Armenian and Syrian Relief." Revenue was split between Selig and the committee. *Ravished Armenia* proved to be an effective vehicle for NER. On its first screening in Los Angeles, it was greeted as a moving, indeed noble story. It opened at Loew's in New York some time later, with Aurora in attendance. Lord Bryce, with many others, hailed the motion picture. (In England it was given another title, *Auction of Saints*.) Some scenes reeking of sexual ravishment offended American viewers. The Pennsylvania Censorship Board initially prohibited the film's showing.[17]

No prints or negatives of the motion picture are known to have survived. Andrew Slide, a cinema historian, has written about it, however; and a book, *Ravished Armenia: The Story of Aurora Mardiganian,* published in 1918, supplies the screenplay. It opens in an inland village on Easter morning, 1915, where the large Mardiganian family is preparing for the forced deportation. On the road Aurora is repeatedly molested. She finally apostatizes in order to save her mother, alas to no avail. At Malatia sixteen girls in the caravan are "crucified" on crude crosses—the most sensational scene in the film. Aurora is finally rescued by the real-life Armenian military hero, General Andranik, and taken to Petrograd, where she embarks on a Norwegian ship for the United States. (Henry Morgenthau appeared in the film as himself.) Aurora Mardiganian, as it turned out, could not accustom herself to the part of a Hollywood star. Indeed, in the film and in public appearances her part was often taken by stand-ins. Several years after the film's debut, she married an Armenian American, raised a family, and apparently died in Los Angeles in 1994.[18]

The international plight of refugees, which bulks so large in the history of the twentieth century, really began in the First World War; and the Armenian genocide, or more particularly the backwash of the genocide, was a substantial part of it. But there were also millions of Greeks, driven from Asia Minor, and of Russians, the residue of the defeated army in Eastern Europe, along with the exiles of the Bolshevik Revolution; and still others set adrift on the turbulent seas of war. Remarkably, the Treaty of Brest-Litovsk, March 3, 1918, by which Germany secured Russia's withdrawal from the war, had a harsh impact on the Armenians in the Caucasus. It turned back to Turkey the formerly Armenian districts of Kars, Batum, and Ardahan, won in the 1878 war, all strategically necessary to the defense of Russian Armenia. An angry pastor of an Armenian church in Troy, New York, wrote in a cogent communication to the *New York Times,* "A great tragedy has been enacted by the murderous Turk, in defiance of all the laws of God and men." Here, too, he thought, was the ultimate proof of German perfidy. The cession of the old strongholds was "the reward which the Turk receives at the hand of Germany for doing a clean job of massacring over a million Armenians in Anatolian Turkey." And now the Turk could slaughter still more.[19]

The three Transcaucasian countries—Georgia, Armenia, and Azerbaijan—entered into a federation. It was too fragile to last, however, as Muslim Tartars, or Azeris, sided with the Turks. An Armenian journalist from Tiflis, speaking to a conference of the Labour Party in London, stated that one-half of the Armenian people in this area, with their homes and property, had been destroyed.[20] Things might have grown even worse but for the arrival of British troops in Baku to enforce the armistice in the Caucasus.

Earlier, on May 30, 1918, Armenia hastily declared its independence. The declaration was woefully premature. Still, it might ensure that brutalized nation a place at the peace table. As the leading authority on these matters, Richard G. Hovannisian, has written, "Thus, the republic was created under conditions so tragic as to defy adequate description. Yet there was an Armenia. In mid-1918 even that was a remarkable accomplishment."[21]

Turkish arms had been routed in the Near East, and the Ottoman Empire, for so long sick and dying, finally expired with the mortifying armistice signed at the island of Mudros on October 30, 1918. The Young Turk leaders took speedy flight. A new sultan, Mohammed VI, mild and submissive, with the countenance of a university professor, according to a London correspondent, apologized for Turkey's part in the war, promised justice to the perpetrators, and expressed regret for the Armenians. Even as he spoke, however, Turkish forces withdrawing from Urmia, in Persia, and from Baku, Oili, and Ardahan, in the Caucasus, continued to massacre Armenians. Henry Morgenthau, speaking at a dinner in his honor in New York, hailed the dawn of Armenian freedom and independence, but warned it was not enough for Americans to say to this people, "Take your new found liberty and do with it what you will." The United States must stay engaged. An army of occupation should be sent to Armenia, and Turkey should be placed under an Allied protectorate. None of these things happened, of course. It was a soft armistice. The straits were opened. Allied troops were a presence in Cilicia and the Caucasus for a time; but Turkish Armenia was never occupied, and the Ottoman state system was left intact.[22]

The armistice opened a new chapter in the work of Near East Relief. Barton, joined by Dodge and Peet, prepared a memorandum to the State Department calling for the union of the six vilayets of Turkish Armenia with the former Russian Armenia into an independent state of United Armenia. The memorandum was forwarded to President Wilson, who was beginning to think along similar lines. At the head of the United States peace delegation, the president very soon embarked for Europe, where he was wildly hailed as a new messiah. Replying to the entreaties of Pope Benedict XV on behalf of the long-suffering Armenians, Wilson stated, "One of my most cherished desires [is] to play any part that I can in securing for that wronged and distressed people the protection of right and the complete deliverance from unjust subjection."[23] NER launched an ambitious campaign for $30 million to meet desperate needs, and at the same time dispatched a special commission under Barton to survey conditions at firsthand. On its way to Turkey, the commission sought advice from the chancelleries in London, Paris, and Rome. Among its members were Harold A. Hatch, who had co-authored a report, "Reconstruction in Turkey"; Dr. J. H. T. Main, president of Grinnell College; Walter George Smith, president of the American Bar Association; and Rabbi Aaron

Teitelbaum, representing the Jewish Joint Distribution Committee. Sailing on January 4, 1919, the commission passed through Paris as the peace conference came into session.[24]

NER's field of operations at that time extended from the Adriatic to the Caucasus and from Syria to Palestine. As the staff of overseas relief workers filled up after the armistice, so did the American Board's staff of missionaries in the Near East; some of them were, indeed, the same persons. At a meeting of its relief committee in November 1918, a decision was made to send out initially 200 workers, of whom an estimated 75 would be reactivated missionaries. The latter, for the most part, returned to the stations whence they came, and they looked forward with some anxiety to what they would find there. John Kingsbury was shocked by what he actually found in Bardizag, not far from Constantinople. "The Gregorian church is a sorry sight. Pillaged of all its oriental adornments, even to the marble on the altar floor, the place is littered with tables, chairs, bedding collected from Armenian houses. . . . The whole reminds one of an East Side junk shop." With his enthusiasm undimmed, George White embarked on the first boat in December 1918 to resume his leadership of Anatolia College, along with direction of the relief effort in Marsovan. The college was a pale shadow of what it had been when it enrolled over four hundred students. Eight Armenian teachers were victims of the massacre, three more died in the war; everything was in disrepair. No matter, White plunged ahead with his plan to add an agricultural school to the complex. Returnees to Harpoot might have been surprised to meet at the door Maria P. Jacobsen, the Danish missionary, who had remained there—the only neutral in the city—throughout the war. She had found shelter for two thousand Armenian women and children and kept them alive on a daily diet of thin gruel.[25]

Before long Maria Jacobsen welcomed to the mission the Smith College Relief Unit, in affiliation with NER. Composed of five alumnae of the Massachusetts college, in classes ranging from 1906 to 1917, and supported by an alumnae fund, they sailed on the U.S.S. *Leviathan* February 16, 1919. Established in 1917 and attached to the Red Cross for work in France, the unit discovered a new calling after the war. Although technically stationed at Harpoot, its relief workers spread out from Erivan to Aleppo. They worked in hospitals and orphanages and, in one instance, a textile factory in Samsoun. They communicated their distresses and frustrations, together with their satisfaction, in the work to friends at home. "Our work," one of the

ABOVE: *American College at Marsovan.* BELOW: *The hospital. Both of these buildings were among the many missionary institutions turned over to the use of the Committee.*

women observed, "is supposed to be for all races, and we do try to make it so, but the Armenains [*sic*] are really the ones who need it most. . . . There is always room for a large work among them."[26]

The peace conference was dominated by the Big Four (Britain, France, the United States, and Italy) and their respective leaders, David Lloyd George, Georges Clemenceau, Woodrow Wilson, and Vittorio Orlando. Wilson had laid out his design for a new world order in the Fourteen Points enunciated in an address to Congress on January 8, 1918, and so great was their influence on world opinion that the Allies were, to a degree, guided by them. The address grew out of an advisory report assembled by a group of academics, journalists, and public figures called The Inquiry, under the direction of Wilson's friend and counselor Colonel Edward M. House. Taken together, the Fourteen Points represented an updating of the traditional American principles of freedom, openness, peace, and fair dealing in international affairs. They called for "open covenants openly arrived at," freedom of navigation and trade, and deep reduction of armaments; and on a soaring note of idealism Wilson envisioned an association of nations to secure the independence and territorial integrity of great and small states alike. One of the underlying principles was the self-determination of nations. Point 12, in particular, said that the Turkish portion of the Ottoman Empire should be sovereign and secure, and that other nationalities under Turkish rule—Greek, Syrian, Arab, Armenian— should be afforded opportunity for autonomous development. This guarantee was no less important to Turkey, which many people thought to divide and dismember, than to the minority nationalities within the old empire. It marked, indeed, the first time the United States had taken a position on the Eastern Question. The principles embodied in the Fourteen Points were roundly stated. Their application to concrete situations was often unclear. Further interpretation of "autonomous development" with regard to Armenia was provided to Wilson before he embarked for Europe. The new republic should be given a port on the Mediterranean and some great nation should be appointed its protector.[27]

A system of mandates was not envisaged in the Fourteen Points; Wilson, however, quickly seized upon it at the peace conference, until it became a fixture of his international outlook. The mandatory system, succeeding to the discredited colonial systems, was established by Article 22 of the Covenant of the League of Nations. Under it a major power assumed, subject to the League, a protective and tutelary role over an emerging new nation for a period of years. The plan was well suited to the government of former German colonies, for instance, as well as to former Ottoman possessions such as Palestine and Armenia. Wilson's secretary of state, Robert Lansing, strongly opposed the mandatory system, believing it a new instrument of Old World imperialism. No sooner had Wilson arrived in Paris than he was importuned to take a mandate over Armenia. Every European power, whatever its charitable professions toward Armenia, dismissed a mandate as an egregious burden, yet urged it on the United States. "It is not too severe to say of those engaged in the propaganda," Lansing wrote, "that the purpose was to take advantage of the unselfishness of the American people and of the altruism and idealism of President Wilson." Wilson's loftiness and high-mindedness, the secretary continued, "blinded him to the sordidness of purpose" of the self-serving diplomats and pretenders gathered at the peace table.[28]

Although Armenia had no seat at the peace table, it was represented in Paris by not one but two delegations. One was appointed by the catholicos, the supreme patriarch of the Gregorian church. Headed by Boghos Nubar Pasha, of an illustrious Armenian family in Egypt, it was designated the "national delegation," and was generally assumed to speak for Armenians in Constantinople, in Cilicia, and in the far-flung communities of the diaspora. The other delegation, that of the Republic of Armenia, was headed

Campaign poster of the American Committee for Relief in the Near East

by Avetis Aharonian, a Dashnak nationalist and revolutionary identified with the former Russian Armenia and the six Turkish vilayets
of eastern Anatolia. Despite differences between the two leaders
and their respective constituencies, they reached agreement on
strategy and objectives and spoke with one voice as the Delegation
of Integral Armenia.[29] Both delegations looked to the United States
for aid and leadership. Aharonian declared to an American diplomat, "Your Wilson came from Washington, but he was sent by
God." Both delegations pleaded for an American mandate over Armenia, yet emphasized it should be the governorship not of a pro-
consul but of a tutor and friend. Morgenthau could recall a long interview with Nubar Pasha in Paris in 1917. Laying out a large map
of the Near East and suggesting the limits of the new nation, he
pleaded for American aid and protection. It would not be arduous
or difficult or prolonged. The Armenians had already learned much
from the Americans and would rapidly become masters of their
own house. "They [the Americans] could do for the Armenians
what they have done for the Philippines." Nubar Pasha also pointed
out the geopolitical importance of an independent Armenia running from the Caucasus to the Mediterranean. It would be "a buffer
state" between Turkey and Russia, and in other directions, Syria
and Mesopotamia, of special interest, respectively, to France and
Britain.[30]

The idea of an American mandate for Armenia took root in
American opinion as the peace conference began. It did not origi-
nate with Near East Relief, though it harmonized with the altruistic rhythm and humanitarian mission of that organization. Its leaders were all sympathetic with the idea, even as they differed on the
form the mandate should take. The first clarion call in Congress
was sounded by Representative Edward C. Little of Kansas in 1918.
Winding up a speech about the distant country, the congressman
concluded with lines from an Armenian poet, Khorene Nar Bey de
Lisignan:

If a scepter of diamonds, a glittering crown
Were mine, at their feet I would lay them both down,
   Queen of queens, Armenia.
If a mantle of purple were given to me,
A mantle for kings, I would wrap it round thee,
   Armenia, my mother![31]

Prominent senators, such as John Sharp Williams, of Mississippi, and Henry Cabot Lodge, Republican chairman of the Foreign Relations Committee, took up the cause. Lodge had introduced a resolution for a self-governing Armenian state. In Great Britain, where Lloyd George, the prime minister, blamed a penurious budget and other hardships of war for Britain's inability to keep the promises it had made to Armenia, Viscount Bryce looked to America to rescue the ravaged land and people. Writing in *Contemporary Review,* he maintained that the United States alone among the powers enjoyed the advantage of a disinterested position toward the struggles of Old World politics, and he underscored its philanthropic record in the Near East. "Its missionaries have already won the gratitude and appreciation of the Christian population, to whose progress they have for the last seventy or eighty years rendered inestimable services by their schools and colleges." Now the Americans had the unprecedented opportunity to bring this labor to a stunning close. Relentlessly Bryce pressed the cause on influential American friends. His last public appearance, in December 1921, was at Mansion House, London, on the Armenian Question, forty-five years since he scaled Mount Ararat.[32]

Among American journals of opinion the *New Republic* was at the forefront in advocating an American mandate for Armenia. It soberly acknowledged the risk that altruism might lead the country astray. The moral imperative in this instance, however, was overwhelming. "If we fail at this juncture to vindicate Armenia's right to freedom we shall never again persuade the world that our moral sentiments are anything but empty rhetoric playing over a gulf of selfishness and sloth." Armenia had no stronger or more persistent advocate than the *New York Times*. In an editorial on February 16, 1919, it recognized that an Armenian mandate ran against the tradition and principles of American foreign policy. "However," the author continued, "a principle is sometimes best recognized by being discarded; and if the country should act under any mandate outside our own neighborhood we should probably be as well satisfied to be in Armenia as anywhere." Armenia, moreover, favored the United States above any other preceptor and protector. The proven capacity of the Armenians was unquestioned. The boundaries of the state remained uncertain; but, as envisioned, it would have access to the sea and the resources to support itself. The editorial pointed out that most of the sufferings of the Armenians were due to the inattention of the Great Powers. "A nation that has been sacrificed for the faith and civilization of Europe should not again be betrayed." The editorial concluded, "Armenia is as much a moral test of the Peace Conference as is Belgium." In subsequent articles and editorials on this subject, the *Times* repeatedly portrayed the mandate as a logical extension of the work of Near East Relief.[33]

President Wilson was deeply conflicted on the question of an American mandate for Armenia. It was not a simple moral conflict, however, but a conflict between what he knew to be morally right and what he calculated to be politically feasible. The son of a Presbyterian minister, Wilson entertained religious sentiments that in other circumstances might have led him into the missionary field in Armenia. Yet when the Turkish massacres began in 1915 and his ambassador plied him with evidence of outrageous crimes against humanity, the president confined himself to ineffectual remonstrance, as Lewis Einstein wrote in the *Nation*, "and to our shame remained apathetic before the most elementary duties of civilization." Later Wilson refrained from a declaration of war against

Turkey, thereby reducing the United States to a minor role in the Near East settlement.[34] The president's indecisiveness with regard to accepting an Armenian mandate also delayed the Versailles Treaty, as well as the Turkish settlement, with deplorable results. Lord Curzon, who as Britain's foreign secretary would later have responsibility for negotiating the Lausanne Treaty, had queried Wilson not long after his arrival in Europe about taking the lead in Armenia, and he replied "that we should lead him a little more slowly up to his fences; that if the League of Nations were once constituted . . . the United States might possibly be less reluctant to consider the question of mandatory intervention."[35] That was fair enough. Wilson was as yet reluctant to commit himself and the American people to an unprecedented responsibility six thousand miles away in the Near East. Returning to the United States in February to attend to the domestic business of his presidency, Wilson no sooner got off the boat in Boston than he made a speech that, in the words of the *Chicago Tribune,* "threw down the glove" in the fight for the League of Nations. He also broached the question of America's duty to Armenia. "Have you," he implored the people, "thought of the sufferings of Armenia? You have poured out your money to help succor the Armenians . . . now set your strength so that they shall never suffer again."[36] Was this not a plea to the American people to shoulder the burden at long term in Armenia?

In Washington, only four days later, Wilson delivered a speech at the White House to the assembled members of the Democratic National Committee. He was unusually candid about the problem of jumping the fence Armenia had become, recalling "an embarrassing moment" in Paris when he was asked point-blank if his country would accept the mandate all the powers had pressed upon it, and he replied offhand it would not. "It wants," he said, "to observe Pharisaical cleanliness." He at once added that as for himself, he was ready to stump the country for it. "Personally," he now confided to his Democratic confreres, "and just within the limits of this room, I can say frankly that I think we ought to." Already the Americans had made a promising beginning in that land. "They know more about Armenia and its sufferings than they know about any other European area; we have colleges out there; we have missionary enterprises. . . . That is a part of the world where already American influence extends, a saving influence and an educating and uplifting influence." He added that an internationalized Constantinople might be thrown into the bargain. In closing, the president warned, nobody is going to get material reward from any mandate there. "It is a work of disinterested philanthropy." This speech, never reported publicly, revealed a president seriously weighing the imponderables of public opinion, national interest, and moral duty as he groped toward a politically sustainable decision.[37]

The Republic of Armenia was not a pleasant land to contemplate in the early months of 1919. It was frigid, violent, and starving. The winter, following upon a season of drought, was one of the worst in memory; 20 percent of the people perished. A *National Geographic* author filed a story, "The Land of Stalking Death," based on a journey aboard an American relief train from Batum to the capital, Erivan. At Tiflis 20,000 Armenian refugees were being fed by NER. At Alexandropol, a city left in ruins by the retreating Turks, the count of refugees had soared to 58,000, and 200 to 250 died daily. Conditions were no better in Erivan. A doctor who had ridden the relief train waved good-bye to the American journalist: "God bless America! For America, with God's help, will do it."[38]

Near East Relief plainly faced a devastating famine in the Caucasus. Herbert C. Hoover, formerly the tough-minded director of the United States Food Administration, took command of European relief. Seeing that Armenia had "only a shadow of a government" and that the slender NER staff at Tiflis was overwhelmed, Hoover intervened there. "If anyone wants material for a treatise

on human woe, intrigue, war, massacre, and governmental incompetence," Hoover later wrote, "he can find ample sources in
the mass of reports from relief officials in Armenia in 1918–1919."
In April he ordered a trusted aide, Howard Heinz, to take charge
temporarily of relief administration. The horror was beyond belief. People were subsisting on grass, if they could find it, and dying
in the streets. Reports of cannibalism were current; indeed, corpses
were exhumed for food. In June Director General Hoover wrote to
President Wilson that 200,000 people had died of starvation. Typhus spread. Hospitals and orphanages filled up. Altogether,
Hoover observed, the reports are "the most appalling that have yet
developed out of [the] war."[39] He made a critical loan of grain to

Armenian refugee women washing grass for the day's meal

help NER over the hump in Armenia, and incidentally to cover a shortage in the recent $30 million fund drive. Hoover also had a part in the appointment of Colonel William N. Haskell as commissioner of Armenian relief. Haskell may have strengthened the administration, though it was never as lacking as Hoover said it was. In his judgment, the administration was nothing less than scandalous— "the greatest human disaster in Europe PERIOD," he told Morgenthau—and he regretted dirtying his hands with it.[40] Haskell himself became a champion of NER. In 1920 he was succeeded by his NER staff officer Captain Ernest A. Yarrow, an efficient and dedicated administrator, long in service in the Caucasus.

Quite aside from the weather, the terrible conditions were made worse by the avalanche of refugees—hundreds of thousands of refugees—from war and genocide returning to the Armenian homeland. They hoped to resume the life they had once known in eastern Anatolia. But, of course, that was a mirage. Turkish authorities were uncooperative, and it was hard to separate the repatriation of Armenians to the lands they had once occupied from current political considerations. A flash of light was thrown on the problem by Dr. Clarence Ussher, the respected medical missionary in Van since 1898. The crash program he proposed called for the immediate return of adult male exiles to the land, with the consent of the government, for the coming growing season, to be followed by women and children. The cooperation of Turks and Kurds would be sought and politics suspended in the interest of repatriation and economic revival. NER would fund start-up costs. The plan struck a responsive chord among diplomats in Paris and in relief quarters; but neither Hoover nor Rear Admiral Mark L. Bristol, the newly installed American high commissioner in Constantinople, supported it. Hoover supposed that 60,000 troops would be required for the operation, and Bristol saw it as an attack on Turkish sovereignty.[41]

Meanwhile, the Republic of Armenia came under attack from unruly Turkish and Tartar armies and assorted brigands. An Associated Press story from Paris, "Turkish Army Moves to Destroy Armenians," appeared on the front page of the *New York Times* on July 31, 1919. This army was not under the sultan but under Mustafa Kemal, the thirty-eight-year-old Young Turk and commander of the Seventh Army, who had set up an insurgent nationalist government at Angora, on the barren Anatolian plateau 200 miles from Constantinople. "Just try to imagine starving people mobilizing for war!" Yarrow wrote dejectedly.[42] Some light is cast on the confusing guerrilla warfare in the area east of Erzroom by the memoir of a British colonel, Alfred (Toby) Rawlinson, *Adventures in the Near East*. Sixty thousand British troops had been in occupation of this vicinity since the armistice. Their withdrawal, scheduled for August, threatened the hopes and even the survival of Armenia. Rawlinson had a special mission: first, to safeguard the railroad from Tiflis to Baku on the Caspian Sea, and second, to demobilize Turkish arms under the Mudros accord. He was an engaging fellow, much taken with "the entrancing beauty" of the country, and cleverly fencing and feinting with the Turkish, Tartar, and Armenian "scoundrels" who surrounded him. Rawlinson was also a great advertisement for Near East Relief. It was, quite simply, "the most practical of all philanthropic organizations." Too little, he felt sure, was known of this "glorious undertaking in the cause of Humanity." The colonel was regularly beseeched by the Kemalist commander Kiazim Karabekir to restrain Armenians from "massacres" of Muslim Turks and Tartars in the country around Olti and Kars. He relayed the complaint in a meeting with three Armenian generals. They did not deny the truth of the complaint, one that Rawlinson averred could doubtless be offset by equally well founded charges on the other side. But the Armenians insisted that the Allies had told them to take possession of the country. To do so they must disarm and vanquish their enemies; and, reported the colonel, "as it could only be done by force, it obviously led to fighting, and fighting as between Moslem and Armenian of necessity led to massacre and atrocities of all kinds."[43]

"Give us this day our daily bread"

As British troop withdrawal, already postponed one month, drew nearer, the United States dispatched a military mission to the Caucasus under Major General J. G. Harbord, the honored chief of staff to General Pershing in France. Nothing substantial resulted, although Harbord submitted a thoughtful report based on his observations. At a dinner marking Harbord's arrival in Erivan, the prime minister, Alexandre Khatisian, could not suppress his fear that "it was the case of a physician so painstaking in diagnosis that the patient died before the treatment could be decided upon."[44] Lloyd George and his government could not be dissuaded from withdrawing Britain's troops in September, despite the obvious danger of creating havoc in the Caucasus. Walter George Smith, the NER commissioner, voyaged to London with a view to changing the British cabinet's mind. He declared, "A wave of indignation will sweep through the United States when it is known that the Armenians have been left to their fate and that American relief workers share the common peril. The cordial relations between the two great English-speaking peoples will be shattered." The British prime minister must have blanched on hearing these words. But the demands of the treasury overruled promise, duty, and compassion for Armenians. The war, Lloyd George declared publicly, had cost Great Britain £40 billion. Moreover, an adverse trade balance had sunk the value of the pound. Demobilization must go forward. Besides, Britain had no real interests in Armenia. "It was," said Bonar Law, chancellor of the exchequer, "an American, rather than a British affair, and the Americans were in a better position to deal with it."[45] That was still an open question. Clemenceau weighed in with his wisdom on the crisis: "France could do nothing; Italy could do nothing; Great Britain could do nothing, and, for the present, America could do nothing. It remained to be seen whether, as a result of this, any Armenians would remain."[46]

President Wilson, after his return to Paris in March, was still in a state of uncertainty about a mandate for Armenia. A potent lobby, the American Committee for the Independence of Armenia (ACIA), had been organized to help him reach the right decision. Actually, as the name implied, it was more interested in Armenian independence than in an American mandate, but its leaders realized that one was believed necessary to the other. The guiding spirits of the committee were two New York lawyers, Vahan Cardashian and James W. Gerard. Cardashian was a veritable Hotspur in the cause of his native land. During the war he had proposed the daring "Cilician Scheme," under which United States forces would go into Cyprus, then under British rule, and from there invade the

Cilician coast, fifty miles away. The idea captured the imagination of Theodore Roosevelt, an ardent, even hawkish Armenophile, but it probably said more for Cardashian's bravado than for his military genius. Any attack on Cilicia, of course, would be an act of war on the Ottoman Empire. Affiliated with the Armenian Revolutionary Federation (Dashnak), Cardashian wrote occasionally for *Hairenik,* the Armenian newspaper in Boston. At the war's close he ran the Armenian Press Bureau for the Armenian National Union. But he soon fell out with that association and its chairman, Marin Sevasly, and started ACIA.[47]

Gerard was from another national and social drawer altogether. Born into a prominent New York family, he became more prominent and much richer by his marriage to the heiress of the Montana copper king Marcus Daly. Gerard, an attorney, had many important clients, among them the *New York World,* the banker Oliver Belmont, and the Wall Street wizard Hetty Green. He was also a leading Democratic politician in the Empire State. President Wilson had named him ambassador to Germany, where Gerard served faithfully and well until the interruption of diplomatic relations. Gerard, the chairman, and Cardashian, the agitator, won an influential following for ACIA, among them the powerful brace of senators—from opposite parties—Williams and Lodge. Wilson, too, paid attention to ACIA.[48]

In its advocacy of an Armenian mandate, ACIA stood for a single national mandate as opposed to any of a variety of plans for a federated or plural mandate embracing the district of Constantinople or perhaps all Anatolia. NER had no official position; but Barton, for a time, had toyed with the idea of a Turkey-wide mandate, then embraced the plan for control over a single but enlarged national state. Both Morgenthau and Caleb Gates, as well as Admiral Bristol, came to favor the plural mandate. In this debate tempers grew warm. Those who spoke for the plural mandate pointed out that almost nowhere outside the present Caucasian

Armenian claims at the Versailles Peace Conference, 1919

republic, thanks to the genocide, were the Armenians a majority of the population, an inconvenient fact that flew in the face of Wilsonian self-determination. Armenian nationalists, on the other hand, called this plan a subterfuge to maintain Turkish domination in the Near East. It would, said Cardashian, "keep the butcher and the sheep together." W. D. P. Bliss, long in service in the Near East, exploded: "Is Armenia never to be free? Is she always to be subject to the Turk? Are Armenians always to be slaves in the hope gradually the Turks will become better masters and not rob, ravish and kill quite so badly?"[49] In the meantime, as Armenia's friends divided on the form of a mandate, Wilson told the Council of Four in Paris that the United States Congress might not approve of any mandate at all.[50]

Gerard made the case for an American mandate over the Republic of Armenia in a feature article in the *Times* on July 6, 1919. He began by saying that after intervention in the European war, historic American isolationism was dead. An Armenian mandate would be earnest acknowledgment of that. Not only was it our humanitarian duty, but it was in keeping with our democratic ideals. The argument proceeded through a long list of reasons. Armenia and America shared a common Christian faith. Among the sixteen new nations to emerge from the war, none had suffered and sacrificed as much as the Armenians. They had, moreover, made substantial contributions to the Allied victory, for instance, by resistance to German forces on the Eastern front. The Armenians looked to us for help, and we were the only disinterested country available to assume the responsibility. The mandate would not be onerous, in part because the Armenians already understood and subscribed

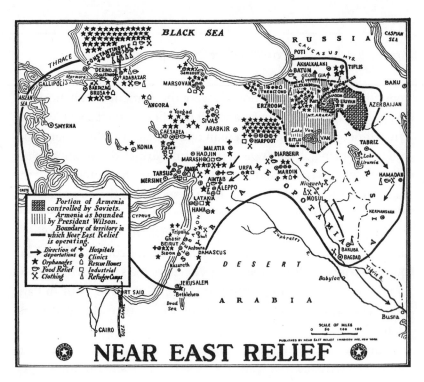

Near East Relief map, 1921

to democratic principles. A small force of U.S. Marines should be sufficient to secure the peace of the country; if not, the envisioned League of Nations would provide necessary assistance. An American presence in that part of the world was an important geopolitical consideration. Finally, Gerard asserted, Armenia would become "the outpost of American civilization in the East." Particularly notable in this long list of reasons for the mandate was the omission of any material gain, whether in commerce or mineral resources, such as petroleum, the United States might secure.[51]

While the mandate hung in the balance, ACIA campaigned for direct aid to Armenia to fill the void that would be left by the evacuation of British troops. Cardashian, in particular, had always favored direct aid and assistance to the Armenian Republic. The country had been compelled to cut its army in half, to 20,000 men. He wished to arm and equip an Armenian national army of Armenian American volunteers. This project would require suspension of the Foreign Enlistment Act. Gerard, unsuccessfully, sought the State Department's endorsement of the effort. The State Department, after all, had not yet taken the first step toward recognition of the new republic.[52]

While Americans debated the mandate question, the peace conference fell into conflict over the distribution of mandates within the generally agreed-upon spheres of interest of the three European powers in the defunct Ottoman Empire. President Wilson, seeking to circumvent secret deals that may have already been made, suggested a joint investigatory commission to resolve the problem. This plan was agreed to in principle, but when the Allies dragged their feet, Wilson sent out the American section on its own. The two American commissioners were Henry C. King, president of Oberlin College, and Charles R. Crane, an industrialist and a trustee of Robert College. Together with a small staff they set out in June for Palestine and the Arab lands of the new Near East. Palestine had an oblique bearing on Armenia. It offered the example of a land with a substantial religious minority, here consisting of Jews, who, since the birth of Zionism in 1896, had settled in significant numbers the ancient lands of the Jewish people, now within the Ottoman Empire. By the war's end they numbered 85,000. In 1917 Chaim Weizmann, a naturalized British citizen, a scientist, and a Jewish leader, forged an Anglo-Zionist alliance when Arthur James Balfour, Britain's foreign secretary, issued the Balfour Declaration, proclaiming Palestine, conquered by General Allenby, a "national home" of the Jewish people. Thereafter Britain assumed a mandate over Palestine. Quite aside from sentiments for the Holy Land as a place of refuge for a persecuted people, Britain was moved by the strategic importance of this land for the security of the Suez Canal and the passage to India. The Jewish homeland would eventually become the state of Israel, and the historian observing its fate cannot help pausing over the utterly different fate of Armenia. It, too, was an ancient fatherland, made fruitful by toil and genius. It, too, was a religious minority that came under the sway of the Ottoman Empire. The two people, Jews and Armenians, were often compared in their national character, their plight, and their aspirations. In history, however, their destinies diverged widely. The American scholar Frank E. Manuel, aware of this anomaly, made much of a small detail in the Ottoman volte-face to accommodate the Jews in Palestine after the abolition of capitulations threatened to subject them to Ottoman law. "While the Armenians were massacred," he noted, "the Zionists were saved."[53] The comparison may be readily extended. Weizmann had no equivalent in Armenia; nor was there any parallel to the political weight of Jewry throughout the world.

The King-Crane Commission acquiesced in the Palestinian fait accompli and went on to Damascus, where the Arab leader, Emir Feisal, anxiously sought to check French ambitions in Syria. The commission also visited Cilicia, claimed for Armenia. It never reached the borders of that country, tagged by Hoover "the poor-house of Europe." In Constantinople, however, the commission held hearings on Armenia's future. Bristol, Gates, and Mary Mills Patrick, president of the College for Women, all testified in favor of a plural, or "integral," mandate of all Turkey, preferably under American auspices. Gates felt that the fate of the Armenians was bound up with that of the Turks, and that a separate state was impractical as well as unjustified. What was impractical, indeed "past human imagination," in the opinion of Mary Graffam, the veteran American missionary in Sivas, was that the two peoples should live together. She observed that about 10 percent of the Armenians exiled from her area four years earlier had drifted back, and more might be expected if self-government was assured. Others, too, Barton and Peet among them, expressed confidence that the eastern vilayets would gradually fill up with Armenians. A professor, K. K. Kirkorian, while recognizing that the Armenians were surrounded on all sides by Islamic peoples, thought this was good reason to establish and sustain a Christian nation as "the only important oasis in the Moslem desert, and in the future struggle of western civilization with the Moslem militarism." Cilicia should be included in this restoration of historic Armenia.[54]

The final report of the King-Crane Commission was highly sympathetic to Armenian claims. The crimes this people had suffered at Turkish hands were "black as anything in human history" and should not be forgotten in the search for a solution to the Turkish problem. At the same time, because of the thinning of the Armenian population in the historic homeland, the territorial pretensions of the proposed state should be scaled back to the former province of Russian Armenia and substantial parts of the vilayets of Trebizond, Erzroom, Bitlis, and Van, where the Armenians might expect to become a majority of the inhabitants in five years or so. The report fell like a stone in Paris; and although it was received by President Wilson, it disappeared from view in the catastrophe that struck his life, coming finally to public notice only in December 1922.[55]

President Wilson returned to the United States in July 1919, immediately after Germany signed the Versailles Treaty. The agreement included the Covenant of the League of Nations, and it alone, in Wilson's judgment, redeemed the treaty from its errors. On July 10 the president laid the document before the Senate. At that moment he may have felt a pang of regret that he had not appointed a leading Republican, perhaps a senator, to the delegation taken to Paris seven months earlier. For the Republican opposition controlled the Senate, and under the Constitution, a two-thirds vote was needed to ratify treaties. As if to add to the problem, the chairman of the Foreign Relations Committee was Henry Cabot Lodge, a man who entertained little but ill will toward the president. Opposition to the treaty centered on the League Covenant and the responsibilities it imposed on the United States in order to implement its system of collective security. The opponents were divided between moderates, like Lodge, who demanded certain "reservations" to protect American interests, and "irreconcilables," who rejected the Covenant altogether. There was room for compromise between the moderates and the president, but his sense of rectitude, like a rod of iron, would not bend. Instead he proposed "to stump the country"—something he had intimated doing on behalf of a mandate for Armenia—to win the support of the American people for an uncompromised League of Nations. The League was finally draped in the mantle of idealism that Wilson had thrown over the war. To those who said he was being obstinate, wrongheaded, or self-righteous, or perhaps questing for martyrdom, he could reply that he was simply being true to his vision of "a world made safe for democracy." On September 4 President Wilson boarded a special train on a 9,500-mile round trip across the country to sell his vision.

In some of his speeches the president reminded his listeners of the nation's obligation to Armenia. Not long after setting forth, he instructed the State Department to get behind Senator Williams's resolution authorizing the president to send troops to Armenia. At Kansas City he appealed to the people to save this long-suffering nation from destruction. Where is the world's pity? he asked. "When shall we wake up to the moral responsibility of this great occasion?" Although he was campaigning for American participation in the League of Nations, the Armenian Question meshed with it. Both questions called upon the American people to shoulder new global responsibilities.[56] On September 26, at Pueblo, Colorado, Wilson suffered a collapse that forced his immediate return to the capital. His health had been a cause of concern for some months; and the collapse was followed one week later by a massive stroke in the White House. It was singularly cruel, for the stroke left him seriously incapacitated for the conduct of his office.

In November the Senate ratified the Versailles Treaty with fourteen reservations to the Covenant. These reservations did not, in the opinion of many observers, impair the workings of the League, nor were they likely to pose a bar to American entry; but the president called them a "nullification" of the treaty. It was soon killed by a combination of Republican irreconcilables and loyal Wilson Democrats. This act was big with fate for the nation and the world. The president once remarked that his heart had formed no habit of failing. Here, with righteous tenacity, he had followed his vision to terrible defeat.

In the interim a Senate subcommittee chaired, under Lodge's appointment, by Warren G. Harding of Ohio, held hearings on the Williams resolution. It stipulated that, whereas the withdrawal of British troops from the Caucasus would leave the Armenians helpless against attacks of neighbors, and whereas the American people were deeply sympathetic with the Armenians, it was therefore resolved that an independent state consisting of the former Russian Armenia, the six Turkish vilayets, and Cilicia should be recognized; moreover, the president was authorized to employ U.S. military and naval forces to secure it. The first witnesses were Armenian Americans engaged in the struggles of their homeland. Despite coaching by Williams, they appeared inarticulate and confused. Subsequent testimony by American diplomatic and relief personnel was effective and on the mark. The armistice had not put a stop to the massacres or the horrors that attended them. A Red Cross officer just returned from Cilicia told of 200,000 Armenian women and children still held in Turkish harems. An army officer who had been on Hoover's staff acclaimed the toughness and heroism of Armenian soldiers. A trio of Near East Relief staffers, Walter Smith, John Main, and Harold Jacquith, all with recent experience in Armenia, argued strongly for American aid and intervention. Main spoke movingly of his experience in Alexandropol: "When I went out on the morning of the 20th of March and walked on the street one block, within the range of my vision four men fell dead from starvation." He submitted a paper he had written, "America's Duty to Armenia," based on his baccalaureate address at Grinnell College in June. In it he said, "America has no right to proclaim her Government as an ideal government unless, when the call comes, she is willing to give expression to it practically to those who need it and want it." Calling for an American mandate, he cited the parable of the Good Samaritan. Senator Williams asked if in his opinion Armenia could carry on alone after the United States withdrew. Main answered in the affirmative, then added that there wasn't "a ghost of a chance" for the country without our immediate help. Why should the United States assume the duty? Williams asked. Main, in reply, pointed to the century-long relationship between the two countries. Britain, on the other hand, had no such relationship.

Jacquith, a young man at the beginning of an impressive career with NER, spoke highly of Armenian grit and honor. The $500,000 a month that NER was expending in that country would reap dividends within two years, he predicted.[57]

As it happened, an Armenian civil mission arrived in the country while the hearings were in progress. After raising the red, blue, and orange Armenian flag in New York, several representatives, together with Vahan Cardashian, appeared before the subcommittee in Washington. One of them detailed the contributions Armenians had made to the Allied prosecution of the war. Cardashian, who introduced a memorandum written by Gerard, was typically forward in speaking of the capabilities and courage of his people. "There is an intense passion on the part of Armenian young men to get into this thing." Alas, they would have to wait awhile. The subcommittee wrapped up its business in the middle of October, but the report, with the resolution, did not reach the Senate floor until six months later, in May 1920. The resolution, moreover, no longer called for the employment of American military and naval forces in Armenia. Although it extended good wishes to that godforsaken country, its only authorization to the president was to send a warship and a force of Marines to secure the life and property of American citizens at the port of Batum.[58] The outcome drove another nail into Armenia's coffin.

The warm greeting extended to the Armenian civil mission prompted the government in Erivan to send a military mission as well. Headed by a true hero, General Jacques Bagratuni, who had lost a leg in battle, it was then joined by a still greater hero, General Andranik Ozanian. The cheering and flag-waving brought out the Armenian American community as never before. In Boston 8,000 people marched from the Commons to a great hall where the floor was a sea of red, blue, and orange and flags draped the stage occupied by 300 Armenian American soldiers. Resolutions calling for the United States' recognition of the infant republic were adopted by acclamation, and the assembly joined in singing the Armenian anthem. Later, at the Copley Plaza Hotel, the dignitaries were honored at a banquet chaired by Alice Stone Blackwell, the prominent suffragist well known to Armenian Americans for her translations of national poems into English.[59]

For all the pressures and all the petitions, the friends of Armenia could not prevail upon the government to extend diplomatic recognition to Armenia, as the European Allies had done. This disappointment undoubtedly sapped the morale of advocates of an Armenian mandate. Their cause was already weakened by the division between those who wanted a single mandate and those who sought a plural mandate. At a great rally for the visiting Armenians in New York's Hippodrome on December 7, the cry was "One nation—one struggle." James W. Gerard, the principal speaker, denounced the so-called joint mandate. It was really a front for "Pan Turanianism"—that is, aggrandizing Turkish nationalism—and it would assassinate Armenia together with Christianity in the Near East. Speaking for the ACIA, Gerard demanded not a United States mandate, which was a cause he no longer thought attainable in view of the president's procrastination and fast-moving events abroad, but rather a strong and independent Armenia from the Black Sea to the Mediterranean.[60]

4 | *Chaos, Carnage, and Survivors*

THE UNITED STATES Senate was in session on March 5, 1920, when William H. King, of Utah, interrupted debate so that he might read a cable from Constantinople just received by Near East Relief: "French troops suddenly withdrew from Marash. Of the 4,500 Armenians who attempted to follow them, 3,000 were massacred and majority of remainder frozen. Also, 16,000 of 20,000 civilians remaining in the city have been massacred." King, who vied with his Mississippi colleague John Sharp Williams for the honor of being the leading Armenophile in the Senate, gravely put his own brand on the shocking news. "The blood of millions of Armenians cries aloud for vengeance; the starving, afflicted, and terrorized people who survive piteously cry out for protection. We are deaf. Europe is deaf. The tragedy continues with leaden eyes and behold its consummation."[1]

Marash was an ancient walled city of Cilicia up against the Amanus Mountains. Before the war some 86,000 Armenians had lived there and in the neighboring villages of the *sanjak,* or district. Cilician survivors of the genocide repatriated in larger numbers than those of the Turkish vilayets to the north, in part because they had not drifted so far from home, and also because of the smaller Kurdish presence there. Near East Relief had a strong position in Marash. Dr. James L. Barton came for a visit, and his organization

confiscated the buildings that had belonged to German business-
men. After the Mudros Armistice, General Allenby and his troops
garrisoned Cilicia.[2] They gave little protection to the Armenians,
however. John H. Finley, then a commissioner for the Red Cross, as
it packed up to leave Asia Minor, tallied the toll of massacred Armenians: "From the town of Aintab," for instance, "30,000 Armenians were driven into the desert to die, and now there are, so far
as we can learn, only 4,000 or 5,000 alive."[3] By agreement among
the Allies, France succeeded to the duty of maintaining peace and
order in November 1919. General Henri Gouraud vowed to do better than the British, and included in his armed force of 6,000 several hundred Armenian volunteers organized as the Légion d'Ori-
ent. This was like waving a red flag before Mustafa Kemal, the
break-away nationalist in Angora.

These events in Cilicia coincided with an inflammatory act by
the Supreme Council in Paris. In order to forestall Italian occupation of Smyrna—the second city of Turkey—which would intro-
duce another power into the partitioning of the Ottoman Empire,
Prime Minister Lloyd George accepted the overture of his Greek
counterpart, Eleutherios Venizelos, to send a large army to take
command of this great seaport more Greek than Turkish in its
composition and culture. Lloyd George seemed spellbound under
the dynamic Greek's charms, pronouncing him "the greatest statesman Greece has thrown up since the days of Pericles." Nor was he
alone in his regard. Harold Nicholson, the British diplomat at the
peace conference, said Venizelos ranked just behind V. I. Lenin as
a world statesman. Another of that class, who managed to dodge
Versailles, Winston Churchill, was shocked by the reckless and violent act of invading Smyrna and augmenting Greek arms in
Turkey. Justice had gone over to the vanquished, he would write,
and the future of the Near East would be forever changed by it.[4]

Kemal's nationalist movement grew up within the fragile shell
of the old regime at Constantinople. One congress after another

succeeded the founding one at Erzroom; and before the end of 1919 a majority of the sultan's old parliament were Kemalists. The outlaw leader of this movement had been crowned a national hero for his defense of the Dardanelles early in the war; but his military talents were eclipsed by the political genius that made him the supreme leader of the new Turkey. With a pertinacity that bordered on arrogance, he forced his will on the Turkish nation. Halidé Ebib, the first Turkish graduate of the women's college in the capital and now a close ally of Kemal, sought to define the secret of his power. It had nothing to do with superiority of culture or intellect. Rather it was his incredible vitality that overwhelmed and dominated everyone in his presence.

> Take any man from the street who is shrewd, selfish, and utterly unscrupulous, give him the insistence and the histrionics of a hysterical woman who is willing to employ any wile to satisfy her inexhaustible desires, then view him through the largest magnifying glass you can find—and you will see Mustafa Kemal Pasha. It was perhaps just because he was a colossal personification of one part of everyday human nature that he had a better chance of controlling the masses than a man who possessed subtler and more balanced qualities or more profound wisdom.[5]

Eventually Kemal would add Atatürk, Father of the Turks, to his name. Remarkably, although his mind was that of a Western liberal statesman, his soul was always that of a Turk.

Aside from the Great Powers, Turkey had two enemies on its borders in 1919–20: the Armenians and the Greeks. Both were Christian, of course, and they had other qualities in common. Both had had a long and generally friendly history in Anatolia. While embattled with the Armenians in the Caucasus, as earlier observed, Kemal was also alert to the danger they posed to Cilicia, on the Mediterranean. The Greeks were thick in the coastal lands behind the Aegean Sea and inhabited the Black Sea littoral, the Pontus, pinched between sea and mountains, and they now seized the opportunity to break into the hinterland. Invading Greeks almost reached Angora before Kemal could secure it. The Greek landing at Smyrna, on the Aegean, in May was part of a campaign designed by Venizelos and his generals to unite the Greeks against Kemal and the nationalists. The prime minister was a Greek irredentist. He had, after all, become a hero in 1913 with the consummation of the reunion of Cyprus, his birthplace, with mainland Greece. Kemal must have been tempted to strike the Greeks at once. He turned first, however, to the more immediate threat of the Armenians— possibly the French—in Cilicia.

"The first major battle in the Turkish War for Independence," it has been written, occurred in Marash over twenty days, January 21 to February 9, 1920.[6] It was often fierce. The Turks laid siege to the city but were driven back by French and Armenian guns. Dr. Mabel Elliott, at the head of the NER hospital, kept a diary of the siege. "We have one hundred and seventy-five persons in our household," she wrote, "patients, employees, and visitors who were here when the battle began." Stanley Kerr, one of her colleagues, eventually became the historian of the battle. On the fifth day he reported that a general massacre of the Armenians was imminent. Some tried to escape. Others, outfitted as Turkish gendarmes, were sent out to Adana with pleas for reinforcements. "All night, Armenians kept coming in with stories of massacre." After their houses were burned they gathered in two big churches. Elliott reflected on the American axiom: Women and children first. "That is because we Americans are so blessedly safe all our lives." And it is wrong. "The first thing Armenian women think of is to save the men and boys." Such is the instinct of race preservation, Elliott added. An airplane flew over and dropped messages. French reinforcements came, and the fighting continued. "One of our nurses learned last night that her two little children are killed." Finally came the stunning news that the French army planned a hasty retreat.[7]

What for the French was a humiliation was for the Armenians a shock of betrayal. Several thousand perished in the fighting or from massacres. Five hundred died in the flames of St. Stephen's Church. Four thousand of the survivors joined the relief column organized to evacuate NER personnel. Kerr stayed behind, but Elliott was among those who trudged into the darkness and through the snow at 10:30 P.M. on the twentieth day. "The swirling snow was so thick that we could see only a few feet . . . ," she wrote. "Four thousand men were trying to get into line, more than five thousand refugees were struggling in the confusion and terror. Screams of horses . . . shrieks of women . . . wails of children . . . creaking gun carriages . . . looming up of camels that grunted and bit." She observed the way Armenian women carried their babies, "holding the two hands against the mother's breast and the child's weight on the bent back." On the third day out, the column lost its way. But then, after a march of about seventy-five miles, a train whistle was heard. "The whole column—thousands of throats—answered it with a terrible sob. A train whistle! Islahai!" Hundreds of the refugees died there. Of the four thousand Armenians who walked out of Marash, only half survived the long march.[8]

Other Cilician cities well populated with Armenians—Hadjin, Aintab, Adana—also experienced siege, massacre, and betrayal in 1920. Hadjin lay about fifty miles northeast of Marash on the slopes of the Taurus Mountains. Four Americans staffed schools and orphanages in this remote place. In April the city came under attack by Turkish soldiers and *chetas* (armed irregulars). They were opposed by 600 Armenian fighters. Although the French had promised to come to the aid of the community, they never did. The American relief workers tried to mediate, without success. The orphans were taken out of harm's way. The standoff lasted until

October, when the Turks brought in heavy guns and reduced the city. Hadjin's Armenian population was decimated. According to news reports, 10,000 lost their lives. At Aintab the Armenians bravely fought the Turks to a standstill. John F. Merrill, president of Central Turkey College—a jewel of American missionary enterprise—wrote, "They had no gunpowder, they made it. They had no grenades, so they made them. They had no bullets. They made them. They even cast a cannon."[9] At Adana, another hot spot, the French and the Turks negotiated a twenty-day armistice without any provision to protect the Armenians. Some weeks later, after fighting resumed, NER felt compelled to withdraw its relief workers, citing dangers arising when Turkish gendarmes took the place of French soldiers. This was a prelude of things to come.[10]

The shock of these sordid events reaching the United States proved a bonanza to NER fund-raising. Barton excitedly wired Peet on March 5, 1920, that at a banquet at the Biltmore Hotel in midtown Manhattan the 700 guests pledged $633,000 in less than one hour. Unfortunately, horror reports from the scene were discounted at the State Department because of the gloss Admiral Mark Bristol, the high commissioner in Constantinople, put on them. While zealous in the performance of his official duties and radiating a deceptive charm on his many callers, Bristol held a venomous prejudice against the Armenians and could not always disguise it in bulletins to his superiors at home. It was his belief that the true facts of events were distorted in the United States to make propaganda for NER and for the Armenians. He opposed their repatriation; and he opposed an American mandate unless it was over the whole of Turkey. The Armenians, he lectured his visitors, were not truly Christians. Nothing was owed to them on that account. When two NER workers, paying their respects, made reference to "Christian martyrs," the admiral returned his usual response: There was no martyrdom among the Armenians; and if the so-called Christian races in this part of the world were Christian, he was no Christian. Armenians were troublemakers; and although he had no choice but to support the work of Near East Relief, he was a less than willing partner in it. Bristol constantly upbraided NER officials for feeding misleading propaganda to the American people. They told only the Armenian side of the story. Bristol's reporting on the massacres in Cilicia disclosed his bias. He compared the Armenian to the fabled small boy who stirred up a hornet's nest, then looked for comfort and protection when he ought to be spanked. "The Armenians have constantly been clamoring for independence when they know that this would arouse the ire of Muslims and the Armenians did not have the force to carry out their desires." The stories of massacres in Cilicia were exaggerated, he insisted. When a subordinate official filed contradictory evidence, the State Department asked for an explanation. The admiral replied that the dire and dismal stories were propaganda on behalf of the Armenians.[11]

The Cilician battles were still in progress when the European allies signed the Treaty of Sèvres, dictating the terms of partition of the Ottoman Empire. The treaty was so severe, and in view of ascendant Kemalist nationalism so out of date, that in modern parlance it was dead on arrival. The treaty explicitly recognized the independence of Armenia and called upon the president of the United States to adjudicate Armenia's amplified boundaries and secure for it an outlet to the sea.

The manifest failure of the Treaty of Sèvres encouraged the French to rid themselves of their unhappy predicament in Cilicia. At a conference in London convened to amend the rejected treaty, alas to no avail, the French prime minister, Aristide Briand, made his own peace with the Kemalist government. France relinquished its claims on Cilicia and at the same time abdicated its responsibility to the Armenians. In exchange it received valuable economic concessions and guarantees from the new Turkey. Although the Grand National Assembly at Angora failed to ratify the accord, it fixed the direction of French policy. "In this way," the historian

Christopher Walker has written, "double-crossed by the French, about 50,000 Armenians were forced out of a land which had been theirs for a thousand years, to become refugees, mostly in Lebanon and Syria."[12] The deal was finalized in June 1921, when the French Foreign Office sent an emissary, Henri Franklin-Bouillon, to Kemal in Angora. The agreement, as Lord Kinross, Kemal's biographer, has said, was nothing less than "a separate peace between France and Turkey."[13]

The Sèvres Treaty posited a mandate for Armenia, preferably under the United States. The Supreme Council, for all its disagreement on other issues, had been united on this one almost from the beginning of the peace conference. President Wilson, as earlier noted, while tending to favor the mandate, was reluctant to commit himself until the American people and the Congress had spoken. The Allied request was renewed in April 1920 at the San Remo Conference, on the Italian Riviera, where the Turkish treaty was drafted by the emissaries of six nations. The United States, having kept its peace with Turkey, was not a participant, but it sent Robert Underwood Johnson, the current ambassador to Italy, as its representative. He forwarded an urgent appeal to President Wilson to assume the responsibility of a mandate over Armenia and also, whatever his decision on that question, to delineate a western boundary for the new country. Johnson, in retrospect, thought it unfortunate that the conference omitted an accommodating modus vivendi for the proposed new relationship between the United States and Armenia. This would have included preparatory arrangements between the two countries, aided and abetted by the Allies, to acquaint the Americans with every department of Armenian government, from defense and finance to health and education. "These wanting," Johnson observed with the gift of hindsight, "she [Armenia] became the prey of Bolshevists and Kemalists and her last end was worse than the first."[14]

President Wilson, ill and distraught, was also bombarded by the

American Committee for the Independence of Armenia with urgent requests, no longer to assume the mandate, which was a lost cause, but to do everything in his power to strengthen the beleaguered Republic of Armenia. Azerbaijan, already absorbed by the Soviet Union, demanded Armenian evacuation of some 5,000 square miles of the mountainous Karabagh district, where 350,000 Armenians were virtually defenseless against but 80,000 Tartars. The republic had desperately sought arms to defend itself but had been frustrated again and again by the British War Office, where it was feared the arms would fall into Russian hands. Gerard forwarded to the White House a cablegram from Erivan stating that in the absence of weapons and munitions, Armenia would be obliged to bow to Azerbaijan's ultimatum on Karabagh, then added his own stinging rebuke: "May I state that had we lent Armenia equipment and supplies for arming forty thousand men, as we repeatedly advocated that we should, the present situation would not have developed. This," Gerard concluded, "is the most grave crisis in Armenian history and unless we hasten to her rescue she will be wiped out by massacre and starvation."[15]

Not long before, in April, after unexplained delay, Wilson had forwarded to Congress the long-awaited report of General Harbord on the Armenian Question. The report caused a stir, yet no one could figure out just what it recommended. It concluded with a listing in parallel columns of thirteen reasons for and against accepting a mandate, followed, curiously, by a fourteenth reason *for* without an opposite. This was a straightforward plea for America to take up "a man's job" that only it could do. The premise seemed to be that the Armenian problem was peculiarly an American problem, made so by America's moral principles and convictions, with which the Armenian people had identified themselves, and its exemplary caretaking role. The mandate Harbord proffered, however, was not limited to the Republic of Armenia; rather it was a "unitary" mandate running from Thrace to the Caucasus. The estimated budget for a five-year period came to $750 million, perhaps 5 percent of the federal budget, and an army of 60,000 American soldiers would be required.[16] Unsurprisingly, the Harbord Report received mixed but generally negative reviews. Herbert Hoover, speaking at Philadelphia, denounced this proposed mandate or any other. The *New York Times,* in an editorial on the report, said "it carried its own rejection with it." Armenia would be swallowed up and forgotten in the mandate it envisioned. Perhaps the time had come to skip the subject and move on.[17]

The American public was, in fact, beginning to tire of the Armenian Problem. The symptoms were part of the growing disillusionment with Wilsonian idealism, with its burden of international responsibility. The florid senator from Ohio, Warren G. Harding, caught the mood when he spoke to a Boston audience in May. "America's present need," he declared, "is not heroic, but healing; is not nostrums but normalcy; not revolution, but restoration, not surgery but serenity."[18] Harding could not then have known that these words would become the signature of his presidency a year later. Public weariness with noble ideals was also being felt at the offices of Near East Relief. People were growing tired of filling a kettle that had no bottom. Clarence Day Jr., writing in the Editor's Drawer of *Harper's Magazine* in 1920, vented his feelings on "the everlasting Armenians." We were at first horrified by the massacres in Turkey, he said. "But as time has gone on, and as the calls of these people for sympathy and friends have continued, a secret annoyance with them has begun to appear. It's an awful thing to say, but they have asked for help so much that they are boring us." And he went on to an anecdote about a pestering "Armenian rug dealer."[19]

The State Department, under a new secretary, Bainbridge Colby, took a more favorable view of Armenia, despite the opinion of Admiral Bristol in Constantinople. The United States extended de facto recognition to the republic in April and received its minister plenipotentiary, Garejian Pasdermadjian, who also went under

the name Armen Garo. Armenia's American friends hastened to
subscribe funds for a legation in Washington, from which the infant nation's tricolor might fly. Wilson, meanwhile, returned to his
old dream of a mandate over Armenia. What prompted him remains a mystery. Perhaps it was the decision to recognize the republic. Perhaps, as Wilson himself suggested, it was the San Remo
invitation. Perhaps it represented his own response to the Harbord
Report. Perhaps it was something as minor as Rabbi Wise's recollection, at the Cathedral of St. John the Divine in May 1920, of the
pledge made to him at the White House as long ago as June 1917.
"'Dr. Wise,'" the president had then said, "'when the war will be
ended, there are two lands that will never go back to the Mohammedan epoch. One is Christian Armenia and the other is Jewish Palestine.'" The proceedings at San Remo, Wise reflected, conferred the Palestine mandate on Great Britain and entreated the
United States to take the Armenian. "In every church, Roman or
Protestant, and every Jewish synagogue," the rabbi fervently declared, "the cry must go up: 'America must save Armenia.'"[20]

The president had again called up the sympathies first aroused
by Ambassador Morgenthau in 1915. As he had recently written to
his friend Cleve Dodge, "I have set my heart on seeing this Government accept the mandate for Armenia. I think it is plainly
marked out for us as the course of duty." He went on to appeal, pa-
thetically, for "some kind of legitimate propaganda," such as Dodge
and NER might supply, to fix the public mind on this project.[21]
About three weeks later, Wilson wrote to Secretary of State Colby:
"It has all along been my purpose to urge upon Congress the acceptance of a mandate over Armenia and I would include Constantinople. What do you think?" Colby replied that such a request
was entirely consistent with the president's record, and it was expedient from every point of view. "At the present time, when the
Allied Powers admit their inability to render any assistance and
solemnly appeal to us, a refusal on our part might involve further

bloodshed, the ruin of the present Armenian Republic, and the opening of the way to further Bolshevism, pan-Turanianism and pan-Islamism in Turkey and in Asia."[22] At the same time, hearing of the president's intentions, James W. Gerard telegraphed Colby warning of the dire effects on Armenia of the Senate's certain rejection of the mandate proposition. "Through my contact with the Foreign Relations Committee and members of the Senate, I know that scheme will fail, and this can give [the] wrong impression to Turks and Tartars that the United States is not interested and thus ruin Armenia."[23] But the president no longer listened to Gerard.

Wilson's message seeking authorization of a mandate over Armenia went to Congress on May 24, 1920.[24] Senator Lodge promptly brought it before the Foreign Relations Committee. Lodge always boasted of his friendship for Armenia and Armenians, and he was on record as favoring an American mandate. But in the crunch Lodge failed to live up to his professions. He had beaten Wilson on the League of Nations and he would beat him here. He may have suspected that Armenia would become the president's back door into the League. At any rate, the committee's resolution declining the request passed after perfunctory consideration, 11-4, on the very day it was offered, May 27. Debate on the floor—it was hurried because the Republican National Convention was about to open in Chicago—disclosed deep divisions on the Armenian Question, which reflected the earlier division on the League Covenant. Washington's Farewell Address, warning against foreign alliances, and the Monroe Doctrine, which apparently barricaded the Western hemisphere from the rest of the world, were paraded before the Senate. Hoover's characterization of Armenia as "Europe's poorhouse" was again heard; senators still could not find it on the map, and wondered why the American people should be taxed to govern and defend it. While one might suppose the altruism of the proposed endeavor would be in its favor, opponents asked what economic interests the United States had in that part of the world.

What was the payoff? The Senate minority leader, Gilbert Hitch-cock, of Nebraska, sought to stay the vote on the resolution in order to amend it in ways that would, by offering direct assistance to Armenia, soften the blow of rejection. To that proposal, how-ever, even Senator Williams, the Mississippi Democrat, voiced op-position. Nothing was closer to his heart than Armenia, he pro-fessed, and he wanted a straight up or down vote on America's friendship for that troubled country. On June 1 he got his wish. The Senate voted 52 for declining the president's request, 23 for grant-ing it, and 21 abstaining. The House Foreign Affairs Committee sub-sequently concurred in this result.[25] A footnote was added nine days later in the Republican platform adopted at Chicago. "We con-demn," the platform declared, "President Wilson for asking Con-gress to empower him to accept a mandate for Armenia." Lodge, meanwhile, laid this gloss on his own conduct: "Do not think that I do not feel badly about Armenia. I do, but I think there is a limit to what they have a right to put off on us."[26]

Two sorts of questions arise concerning President Wilson's conduct on this great issue. The narrower one concerns the May 24 request to Congress. Why did he make it when he well knew it would be soundly defeated? And might have guessed the adverse impact that Gerard suggested. The larger question addresses the failure of his policy on Armenia over a period of years. Here there appears to be a gap between his profession and his performance. Had he chosen to jump the traces of American public opinion ear-lier, say in the first month or so of the peace conference, and pledged the nation at once to embrace a mandate, then rallied pub-lic opinion for it, he might have prevailed. In a thoughtful editorial, "Testing Our Altruism," two days after the president's special mes-sage to Congress, the *New York Times* said the nation's response would surely have been different had the proposition been offered eighteen months earlier. Then it would have expressed untainted and unclouded humanitarian benevolence. Cynicism had yet to set in. And the world had yet to be rocked by prodigious changes. The march of events, however, threw up obstacles and distractions that changed the face of the Near East. The new reality was the Bolshevik Revolution in Russia and the nationalist insurrection in Turkey. "Meanwhile," the editorial continued, "altruism has been denounced as un-American, and if that view is not generally accepted, altruism in foreign policy has yet been condemned as a nefarious attribute of the Democratic party and thrown into the turmoil of a Presidential campaign." In the opinion of isolationist Republican senators, such as William E. Borah of Idaho, "the Good Samaritan was a fool to run the risk of being blackjacked." And so the Senate was content to pass a resolution to show the flag in Batum. The only good result of the mandate proceeding, the editorial concluded, had been to puncture the illusion that the American people were the most righteous on earth.[27]

The president's timing was unlucky not alone with regard to American opinion and politics but also because it postponed the Turkish treaty until the balance of forces had radically shifted in the Near East. Among British and French leaders it became common to blame Wilson for the setbacks they had suffered. It was said that he had misled the Allies, causing them to believe the United States would, in all probability, assume a mandate over Armenia. The historian Thomas A. Bryson has refuted this allegation. Wilson never intimated or promised that he would shoulder this burden, always saying it depended on the will of the American people. Even so, Bryson admits, it is hard to explain why it took him so long to reach a decision on the matter.[28]

The failure with Armenia was but one example of the flawed visionary idealism that President Wilson brought to international politics in general. An American mandate in the distant Caucasus remained a fantasy, it might be argued, unless it was firmly grounded in American national interests. No national interest was ever demonstrated, however. By 1920 American business was only awakening to economic opportunities in the Near East, and most of them lay in directions other than Armenia. As Wilson had suggested in his letter to Dodge in the spring, he had thus far been remiss in educating the American people on the nation's stake in the survival and freedom and prosperity of the Armenians. He had failed in this instance to mount the bully pulpit in the manner of Theodore Roosevelt for something he truly cared about. It was a little late in the day to correct that failure. Dodge, in any event, could not help him, for NER abstained from politics.

Finally, Wilson's illness must be reckoned with. He had suffered a cerebral hemorrhage; his left side was paralyzed. All the evidence, however, suggested his mind was clear. The American people knew very little of his condition. The Constitution was silent on the matter of presidential disability. Into the breach stepped Edith Bolling Wilson, the president's wife, assisted by his faithful personal secretary, Joseph Tumulty, who together made decisions after ad hoc communication with the president. When Secretary of State Lansing undertook to act for the president, he was summarily dismissed. Ray Stannard Baker, Wilson's biographer, told of a Sunday visit to the president in March 1920. Dinner was preceded by movies. He said Wilson's mind was alert but his appearance was dreadful: "A broken ruined man, shuffling along, his left arm inert, the fingers drawn up like a claw, the left side of his face sagging frightfully. His voice is not human: it gurgles in his throat, sounds like that of an automaton."[29] What bearing the president's condition may have had on his actions with regard to Armenia it is impossible to say, but it seems likely the disability affected everything he did.

Certainly Wilson had not lost his fighting spirit. When Senator Carter Glass, of Virginia, called at the White House before the Democratic National Convention in San Francisco, he found the president still hopeful of doing something for Armenia. As Glass was going out the door, Wilson handed him an envelope saying he wanted to get the enclosed into the party platform. The senator, who was the president's choice to chair the convention's Resolutions Committee, opened the envelope on the train. He found it to be a declaration for the Armenian mandate, already rejected, on grounds of Christian duty and humanitarian privilege. That appeal was not incorporated in the platform, Glass later explained, because of strenuous objections from Thomas J. Walsh, of Montana, although a resolution expressing deep sympathy for the people of Armenia was included.[30] In the course of the campaign to come, Republicans denounced it as irresponsible.

President Wilson's last important duty on behalf of Armenia was to adjudicate a new western boundary predicated on the addition of substantial parts of the vilayets of Erzroom, Trebizond, Van, and Bitlis, providing as well for unimpeded access to the sea, all in accordance with the Treaty of Sèvres. Here again there was an unfortunate delay, though the president was not at fault. He sought the expert counsel of a small committee headed by Professor William L. Westermann, who had been chief of the Western Asia Group of the American Committee to Negotiate Peace. Drawing a serviceable boundary over the ragged terrain of eastern Anatolia was not easy work. Kemal pushed his conquests in the area in order to make the task even more difficult. Westermann recommended, with the president's approval, a boundary from Kerason, on the Black Sea, southeast to the Persian border. It added 60,000 square miles to the projected state based in Erivan and made a large addition to its population, an estimated 40 percent of it Armenian, which was expected to increase through repatriation. Alas, it was all a futile exercise. By the time the report was dispatched to Paris, on November 24, Armenia had virtually ceased to exist. Kemal's army controlled the western portion of the newly awarded lands, while the Soviets extended their dominion in the Caucasus. "President Wilson has built a castle in the air," a British diplomat remarked. Admiral Bristol, with his customary disdain of Armenia, thought to observe that the boundary award had placed the president in the "false position" of serving the advance of Bolshevism. The *New York Times* chimed in with the tragic reflection that the empty award, in the end, should be President Wilson's monument. It had, the editor opined, "a sort of melancholy historical interest."[31]

On December 4, 1920, Joseph Stalin, commissar for nationalities in the Soviet Union, successor to the empire of the tsars, extended greetings to the people of its latest conquest: "Armenia weary and much suffering, delivered by the favor of the Entente and Dashnaks back to famine, destruction, and flight, deceived by all its friends: Armenia now consecrates her deliverance in that she declares herself a Soviet country."[32]

The promises of all its Western friends unfulfilled, left to the choice of a protector it knew too well and the revolutionary star in the firmament, Armenia reluctantly submitted to the Soviet Union. In retrospect, the result seemed foreordained, but, like most great historical turning points, it came at the end of a winding road. In the fall Armenia was at war with the nationalist government of Mustafa Kemal at Angora. As the uncontested president of the national assembly, Kemal was the virtual dictator of the "counter-government." His commander on the eastern front, Kiasim Karabekir, strained at the leash to attack the hated Armenians. Kemal's National Pact called for the recovery of the eastern provinces of Kars, Ardahan, and Batum, which, indeed, the discarded Brest-Litovsk Treaty had promised to return to Turkey. Karabekir was turned loose on September 13, 1920. Kemal had secured himself against Soviet opposition by initialing a treaty of friendship in Moscow. The tsarist and Ottoman empires had been inveterate enemies. Now both had yielded to new anti-imperialist and revolutionary governments, and regardless of the differences between them, each found reasons for opportunistic collaboration. Each sought to bait the Allied Powers. Each, in seeking its own interest, selfishly used the other. Kemal, for his part, sought to eliminate the danger from Armenia in order to concentrate on the greater threat of Greek conquest in Anatolia.

Helpless to stem the assault of Turkish arms, Armenia suffered one humiliating defeat after another. The fall of Kars at the end of October was widely attributed to treachery and incompetence on the part of the defenders. The trail of massacre and ruin reached as far as Alexandropol, Armenia's second city and a center of Near East Relief operations. It was sacked and occupied by Turkish invaders. "The Armenian population of Alexandropol, and of some tens of towns of Armenia have been put to the sword," one observer wrote.[33] The Treaty of Alexandropol, signed at midnight December 2, was the crushing blow. It stripped the country of what little military capability it had left and fixed the new western boundary at the Araxes River. That placed Mount Ararat, the nation's symbolic landmark, in Turkey. Armenia was compelled to declare the Treaty of Sèvres null and void, and to recall its envoys from Europe and America. Refugees forfeited repatriation rights after one year. Yet, as harsh as the treaty may have been, its significance lay in the past, for it was never ratified, as it was at once superseded by the Sovietization of Armenia. Georgia, the last of the Transcaucasian republics, soon followed Armenia into the Soviet Union.

Under the force of these events, Armenia's fortunes in international diplomacy rapidly crumbled. After the United States rejected the proffered mandate, rumors occasionally surfaced that another country—Canada, Norway—might take it up; but they proved ephemeral. Some spokesmen among the Allies thought the League of Nations should assume the responsibility. The League secretariat would not touch it, however, nor would the Republic of Armenia even be admitted to the League in the absence of defined boundaries. At the first meeting of the Assembly of the League of Nations in Geneva, in November 1920, just before the Soviet takeover, Lord Robert Cecil and René Vivani, of Britain and France respectively, proposed appointment of a commission to draw up plans to aid Armenia. Nothing came of this proposal, though an invitation was extended to President Wilson, after his work on the boundary, to mediate the conflict between Kemalist Turkey and Armenia. He agreed, provided Henry Morgenthau would be his deputy. Morgenthau, who had become a roving ambassador on many fronts, complied. He seemed to think there was still hope for Armenia. After the Soviet takeover, he argued that the Allies, including the United States, should strike a deal with the Soviet Union: in exchange for U.S. diplomatic recognition of the new regime, it would undertake to save and succor Armenia. To this idea the editor of the *New York Times* snapped: "The Armenian question has long since passed beyond the stage of moral influences."[34] It may also have passed beyond the stage of diplomatic mediation. The real mediator was not Wilson, not the League of Nations, but V. I. Lenin.

Meanwhile, the American Committee for the Independence of Armenia, ever devoted to the republic born in 1918, continued its agitation. The Sovietization of the client state was a severe handicap, however. A rival organization, the American-Armenia Society (formerly American Friends of Armenia), soon began advocating a different idea, an Armenian National Home, the brainchild of George R. Montgomery. He had refined it in discussions with Boghos Nubar Pasha, with Walter George Smith and other American Armenophiles. Montgomery, a lawyer and a diplomat, the son of missionaries, knew the Near East well. The homeland idea was suggested by Zionist Palestine, of course. Part of the genius of the Balfour Declaration was that it did not premise an eventual Jewish state, rather a homeland, which was less threatening to the Arabs. France's tentativeness about a mandate over Cilicia seemed to open a similar opportunity for the Armenians. The little matter of Kemalist conquest of the proposed homeland, to which it was hoped Caucasian Armenia, currently under the Bolshevik heel, would in time be adjoined, seemed to present no obstacle. The idea can be described only as surrealistic. Nevertheless, it assuaged multiple guilts and disappointments over Armenia. The American-Armenia Society attracted a substantial following, though it never replaced the leadership of ACIA.[35]

In 1920 Near East Relief operations were organized in three geographical divisions: Constantinople and Anatolia, Syria and the Levant, and the Caucasus. The Syrian division, at Aleppo, under Bayard Dodge, son of NER's treasurer and a professor in the university at Beirut, was the smallest of the three, though rising numbers of Armenian refugees and orphans made their way there. Constantinople, always a magnet for Armenians, was flooded in November with 120,000 Russian refugees, the remnants of General Petr Wrangel's White Russian army in the Crimea. They presented difficulties to NER's mission.

The Caucasus was the largest of the three divisions. In the summer of 1920, NER's news bulletin, now called *New Near East,* contained a consolidated monthly report of relief activities in the Caucasus. The area was divided into eight districts, of which the most important were Erivan, Kars, and Alexandropol. Overall there were

- 81 orphanages, with 20,779 orphans
- 43 hospitals, with 5,530 beds
- 58 clinics and ambulatories

The relief accounting, with certain other activities, ran as follows:

- 19,851 adult refugees on relief in camps, barracks, etc.
- 55,039 children fed at soup kitchens
- 561,970 refugees aided by rations of bread, flour, and soup
- 14,525 children attending schools
- 14,862 children employed in NER industries.[36]

Nearly all of this relief was dispensed to Armenians. The money had been raised from the American people for Christian Armenians and Syrians, not for Turks or Russians or even Greeks, though the latter had the Orthodox faith in their favor. Admiral Bristol complained of the discrimination, but, knowing his feelings toward Armenians, NER officials paid no attention to him. The Syrians alluded to in the organization's original name were, in fact, the Christian Assyrians, sometimes called collectively the Church of the East, or Nestorians, mainly in the Persian lands of ancient Urmia. Now

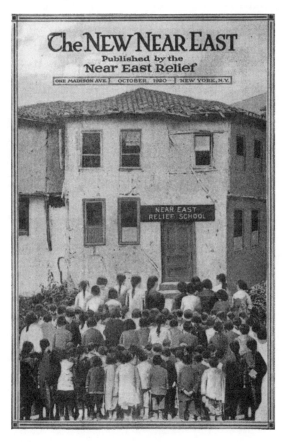

Cover of The New Near East *showing school-children, October 1920*

numbering 40,000, they were currently fed and sheltered in British refugee camps, but NER's Caucasian division would assume responsibility for them in April.[37]

Captain Ernest A. Yarrow succeeded Colonel William Haskell, Hoover's appointee, in the administration of relief in the Caucasus on August 1, 1920. He was NER's director general in that part of the world, and except for a brief leave in the United States for public speaking, he remained on the job for six years. Born in England, Yarrow had emigrated and later graduated from Wesleyan College, in Connecticut. He came by his military title, curiously, in the Spanish-American War. During the World War he had served in the Red Cross. In 1919 he had seen the worst of the famine in Armenia. In the fall of the next year he faced a crisis of another kind. As NER's Charles Vickrey had predicted, the harvest of 1920 largely overcame the famine. It supplied Armenia enough food for seven to eight months. A relief worker, Blanche Knox, just returned to Alexandropol after eighteen months' leave at home, remarked, "When we arrived there early in 1919 conditions were horrible." Now she saw a different city. "The streets were cleared and the people well clothed in old American garments or in suits made at NER industrial shops."[38]

Then came the Turkish invasion and reconquest of Kars and Ardahan. Armenia, with little enough land to feed its own people, let alone tens of thousands of hungry refugees, suddenly lost the fertile lands to the west. The relief workers in Kars, with several thousand orphan children to feed, were cut off from supplies of grain. Yarrow gave all NER personnel the choice of leaving the Caucasus. Many did so. The Soviet takeover aggravated the difficulty. The Turks, at least, were a known quantity. Bolshevik commissars, dedicated to revolutionary social and economic change, were a new and alien breed. Would they accept a bourgeois American relief organization staffed by bourgeois American men and women? The Alexandropol treaty returned that important city to

Armenia, but Yarrow, upon the arrival of the Bolsheviks, preferred to operate from Kars. It was accessible, although through Turkey, while the railroad from Batum, via Tiflis, was frequently interrupted. Writing to the commissar of Alexandropol, Yarrow said he regretted the withdrawal but felt it was impossible to remain. "There was a persistent and almost violent expression of suspicion regarding the purposes for which the NER had come to Armenia. It was constantly hinted that the plain humanitarian motives actuating us were simply a cloak for some deep and sinister political intrigue." Moreover, members of the staff were threatened with seizure and imprisonment.[39] When the political climate improved, Yarrow returned operations to Alexandropol. Among its advantages were the abandoned Russian army barracks, which NER would turn to new uses as warehouses, hospitals, and orphanages.

Rail communication with Batum remained a problem for several months, however, for the port was sometimes closed. A relief worker told of her experience. "On the morning of April 22, 1921, . . . we had one half day's ration of flour for the orphanages and a few beans and rice. It was not possible to further reduce the ration. We simply had to issue it and then, for the following day, we planned to use for the children what American personnel commissary supplies we had left and after that—nothing." In desperation, she with some companions trekked to the railroad station to meet an incoming train. When it drew in, miraculously, a uniformed American jumped off, saluted, and said, "'I have two cars with supplies for Near East Relief.'" The relief worker cried unashamedly.[40] Duty in Alexandropol, presently renamed Leninakan—today called Giumri—remained hazardous throughout the early months of 1921. The Bolshevik government, unrecognized by the United States, did not honor American passports. "All foreigners were potential enemies," Barton later wrote of this time. "They could not appeal to any government except the Soviet authorities for protection, and as long as they remained in the country, they were subject to Soviet laws. . . . For some weeks the future of the relief work hung in the balance, with the weight of thousands of helpless, hungry orphaned children dragging on the scale."[41]

With the spring came a thaw not alone in the weather but in relations between NER and the local government. Yarrow ingratiated himself with the authorities, and in the course of newly found amity, a comprehensive agreement was negotiated between the Soviet Republic of Armenia and the NER. The former recognized the latter as a wholly humanitarian organization, as defined in its congressional charter. Its abstention from politics and from pursuits of commercial or financial gain was acknowledged. In seeming defiance of Marxist teachings, the accord accepted NER on its own terms: a voluntary organization actuated by "the spirit of human brotherhood." All this being so, the government announced its desire to cooperate fully. It confirmed "the tenancy and unhampered occupancy and use . . . of all houses, land and other properties now occupied or used by Near East Relief, or that may hereafter be allocated to the Near East Relief." Freedom of residence and of travel was accorded to NER personnel, including ingress and egress at ports of entry. Supplies were to be admitted duty free and their transit by land was given without charge. It was altogether a remarkably liberal agreement. Yarrow must have taken great satisfaction in communicating it to the State Department. James L. Barton, a man not given to easy praise, congratulated Yarrow for an agreement that was "little short of a triumph." People were incredulous upon learning that he had won the cooperation and support of the Bolshevik authorities for American relief work.[42]

By June 1921 Yarrow had implemented his plan to concentrate all the orphans under his jurisdiction in Alexandropol. At the peak they numbered 25,000, and Alexandropol, or Leninakan, was known as Orphan City. One building alone, the Polygon, accommodated several thousand. Every month Orphan City consumed

The 30,000 inmates assemble on the playground of the Orphan City at Alexandropol

enough food—2,300 sacks of flour, forty barrels of lard, 1,900 cases of evaporated milk, and so forth—to feed a small army. To this uniquely fascinating hospice for waifs of war and devastation came a new worker, placed in charge of the hospital, Dr. Mabel Elliott, earlier encountered in Marash. After escaping through the snows of Cilicia, she had taken a brief leave in the Unites States, then continued her Near Eastern odyssey in Ismid—ancient Nicomedia— near the Bosporus, where she directed a new hospital under the auspices of American Women's Hospitals, one of the important volunteer agencies thrown up by the Great War. The hospital was staffed, supplied, and operated by NER. Three months after Kemal's army came into control of Ismid, Elliott was reassigned by NER to the Caucasus. Her book, *Beginning Again at Ararat,* is perhaps the best personal memoir from the pen of a leading NER worker in the field. Struck by the human story that was really 25,000 children's stories, Elliott also marveled at the scale of it all:

> Often it seemed that the big fantastic spectacle was this ad-
> venture of American organization in the immemorial chaos
> of the Caucasus. It was a bit of modern America inserted be-
> tween two chapters of the Old Testament—the wandering
> refugees led by Moses, the wars between Israelites and
> Philistines, the Lost Tribes in their dispersion, coming sud-
> denly upon a gigantic American business organization which
> handled food and shelter and education and hospital care.[43]

It was truly more American than it was Armenian or Soviet Com-
munist.

At times, however, Orphan City became a testing ground between two systems, American and Bolshevik. When Esther Pohl
Lovejoy, the general director of American Women's Hospitals, arrived there late in 1921, the Armenian workers in the hospitals were
on strike over the firing of five of their comrades. Whose rules
should apply? The workers' union won this contest, and the Armenians were reinstated. As she studied the Orphan City, Lovejoy
came to think of it as "a social experiment station, an isolated lab-
oratory in which Armenians and Americans were conducting an
important experiment in the communistic scheme of life." It was
manifest in education, child welfare, agriculture, health care, and
countless other avenues. "American money and efficiency combined with Armenian tenacity of life and purpose constitute a
strong alliance," Lovejoy wrote.[44]

Near East Relief activities in Armenia ranged over a wide field.
As the number of children in orphanages soared, the Executive
Committee in New York adopted a modified program designed to
reduce the number institutionalized. Wherever possible the orphans would be returned to relatives qualified to care for them; or

they would be placed with unrelated families of the same nationality and religion, with provision for continued access to hospital care and other aids. The twofold aim was to bring children back to conditions of normality as quickly as possible and to give them the educational equipment they needed to become self-sufficient by age sixteen. Many of the orphans had been so badly scarred mentally and emotionally that they had forgotten their names, their language, and where they came from. For some, remembrance of the horrors of deportation and massacre blocked out everything else. In 1922 NER appointed a child welfare professional to set up clinics intended to treat such problems. Her name was Frances McQuaid; and she recruited thirteen Armenian girls with American missionary schooling and trained them to become visiting child welfare workers.[45] Many of the children suffered from debilitating diseases, the most common being trachoma, a painful and infectious malady of the eyes. "Leninakan might better have been named 'trachoma city' rather than an 'orphan city,'" Lovejoy wrote. One-third of its young denizens were afflicted with the disease at one stage or another. One of the Russian barracks was renovated to confine the sickest patients, and it quickly filled up with 6,000. Research on the disease was carried on at NER's Trachoma Hospital in Constantinople. It had 336 beds and was staffed by one American and two native physicians, four Armenian nurses, and sundry aides.[46]

Education was slanted toward the development of industrial and vocational skills. For girls these skills typically were sewing and handiwork. The best products—fancy needlework and embroidered linen and lace in traditional designs—were sent to the United States for sale at Christmas and Easter. Young boys learned such trades as shoemaking and tailoring. As boys grew older, the lucky ones were apprenticed as farmers. In the fall of 1921 the Soviet government made available to NER 17,600 acres of land for farming. This was a boon. (Some months before, a concession of 6,000 acres in Thrace had been obtained from the Greek government.) After the next harvest NER allocated $100,000 to buy seed grain with a view to reviving agriculture among the Armenians. Men, refugees who thus far had received few benefits, could rejoice in this development. A special train of thirty cars loaded with farm machinery arrived in 1922. The first 1,000 acres were plowed in eleven days by ten American tractors, a feat, it was said, that would have required 1,000 oxen and 500 men by age-old methods in Armenia.[47] Another facet of the agricultural revival was the reclamation under NER auspices of 16,000 acres of cotton, rice, and grain land along the Araxes River, known also as Garden of Eden River for its proximity to Ararat. William A. Biby, NER's agricultural expert from Kansas, rhapsodized on this bonanza:

> I have seen—
> corn twelve feet high
> wheat tall enough to hide a walking man.
> rich, black soil nowhere less than a yard deep.
> hydraulic power possibilities enough to irrigate production
> beyond men's dreams.

What a pity, Biby thought, that the United States turned down a mandate of, potentially, "the future garden spot of the world."[48]

The wells of American charity, however, were beginning to run dry. Yarrow, upon hearing news of retrenchment from NER headquarters, was deeply disappointed. "For the first time since the beginning of the war," he cabled in response, "I have hope of the economic regeneration of Armenia."[49] He had a plan to relocate refugees in the villages and supply them initially with the wherewithal of survival. This plan responded to the maturing population of orphans and also cut costs. American support for relief in the Near East was not limited to cash contributions, though that was of first importance, from the donations of public schools—$175,000 in 1920—to the munificent gifts of philanthropies. But there were also in-kind gifts, such as 25,000 pounds of cocoa courtesy of the

Hershey Chocolate Company, as well as freight charges waived by railroads. The annual old-clothing drive in May, culminating in Bundle Day, June 1, had U.S.A. written all over it. Armenian children and adults had come to depend on it. Another accessory form of relief was the individual remittances program managed by NER. By November 1921 a total of $2,330,979 had been routed from Armenian Americans in the main to refugees in need in the Near East.[50]

While the Caucasus was the focus of NER work after the armistice, it should not obscure the larger picture. A map printed in *New Near East* in February 1921 showed the facilities in Soviet Armenia, then expanded to the Armenia as bounded by Wilson, then from Nineveh (Mosul) to Baghdad in the valley of the Tigris River, then swept through Syria to Jerusalem—the most southerly point—and Cilicia northward to the Anatolian plateau, rapidly falling under the sway of Mustafa Kemal, where Harpoot was the center of operations, finally to Constantinople.[51] (See p. 138.) The Armenian population of Anatolian Turkey in 1921 was estimated at 561,000 and rapidly declining, compared to 1,293,000 in the Soviet republic. Kemal's army continued to massacre Armenians, primarily in Cilicia, and increasingly Greeks from the Pontos to the Smyrna coast. In June 1921 *New Near East* reported 31,500 deaths of Christians in authenticated massacres by the nationalists during the last eighteen months.[52] Admiral Bristol had no patience with appeals made on behalf of Armenian victims of the latest Turkish enormities. "I believed," he told NER's Harold Jaquith, "it is just as bad to steal five cents as five dollars, and in the same way it was as bad to massacre hundreds or massacre thousands or even millions."[53]

Jaquith was NER's director at Constantinople, where everything was in a boil. The authority of the Ottoman regime had broken down, and change with all its apprehensions filled the air. "In the scented gardens of the haremlik where once the chosen ones disported themselves on the pleasant afternoons," one wrote, "they are now playing football." "They" were the orphans in the care of

Near East Relief.[54] At the Scutari orphanage on the Bosporus—a place remembered for the compassion of Florence Nightingale— the children made a presentation to the American relief workers:

> May we not consider ourselves a little part of America? We have only lived because America has fed us. We have been kept alive and grew up on American milk. American flour gave us bread when we had no other. Our soup has been made with American beans. Your flag has been the only flag to help us and our hearts are American. Our bodies are American without a country. May we think of your land as our adopted home at least? When we sleep at night we are in American beds under American blankets. When we are awake we talk of America and study in the books you have sent us. Although the Star and Crescent floats over Turkey, we see only the large white star of Near East Relief and the many stars [of] the dear American flag.

If any of these children were eventually to immigrate to the United States, they were almost Americans before they got off the boat. No wonder that Dr. Elliott could say, "Something of America has been planted here; something that will grow."[55]

5 | *The Great Betrayal*

IN THE BROAD DAYLIGHT of the Ides of March, 1921, on a street in the Charlottenburg district of Berlin, a large man in a greatcoat, carrying a walking stick, was shot in the head from behind and died instantly. The assailant, a young man, threw down his gun and ran, but was quickly apprehended by passers-by. He put up no resistance as he was taken to the local police station. The identity of the victim was soon established. He was Mehmet Talaat Pasha, formerly grand vizier and head of the war cabinet of the Ottoman Empire, who on November 1, 1918, had fled Constantinople with his closest associates and finally taken refuge in Berlin. His assailant was a twenty-four-year-old Armenian, Soghoman Tehlerian, who described himself as an engineering student. Freely confessing to the crime of premeditated murder, he said that since December he had been in pursuit of Talaat, the man he held responsible for the massacre of his family.[1]

In June Tehlerian was brought to trial in a Berlin criminal court. Interrogated by the judge in the presence of a jury, Tehlerian told the story of the forcible deportation of his family from Erzinjan in 1915: of how the men were rounded up and shot, of the ordering of the caravan and the wanton abuses by the gendarmes. When a sister was dragged away and raped, his mother screamed, "May I be stricken blind!" A brother's head was split by an ax; his mother was shot; and he, the young son, had been left for dead, yet survived to make his way back to Erzinjan late in 1916, only to find it abandoned and in ruins. Seeking to understand the defendant's motives, the judge asked what he felt after shooting Talaat. "I felt satisfaction of the heart," Tehlerian answered. The judge continued, "Does the custom of blood revenge exist among the Armenians?" And Tehlerian answered firmly, "No." His attorney, appointed by the Dashnak party, called Dr. Johannes Lepsius, the German advocate of the Armenians, as the primary witness. The documents he had assembled on the genocide were allowed to speak for themselves. Corroboration was then offered by Armin T. Wegner, who as a soldier in the German Sanitary Commission in 1915 had made an extensive photographic record of the genocide as he had witnessed it in the Mesopotamian desert. Tehlerian suffered from epilepsy but no claim of mitigation was made on that account, nor was any plea entered for what today might be called "temporary insanity." Tehlerian was content to rest his case on a Dostoevskyan paradox: "I have killed a man but I am not a murderer." The jury believed him, returning a verdict of not guilty after one hour's deliberation. The verdict ran against the murdered man rather than his assassin.[2]

Tehlerian sailed immediately for the United States. This was not his first visit; he had gone there in 1920. There Armen Garo, also known as Garejian Pasdermadjian, the erstwhile plenipotentiary to the United States, enlisted the young man in the underground enterprise Garo at first called "The Debt" but that came to be known as Operation Nemesis. It targeted seven of the foremost CUP leaders of the wartime genocide, including the cabinet triumvirate in Constantinople, for assassination. Now, a year later, his own mission completed, Tehlerian arrived in New York City a cathartic hero of Armenian Americans. Edward Alexander, who would later write a book on the subject, could recall from childhood going with his father to the Armenian church on 27th Street to do honor to a young Armenian, just arrived, whom the men felicitated with tones of gladness while the women vied to kiss his hand. Why? the boy asked. "Because with that hand he avenged our people. Never forget him!" the father replied. The hero was, of course, Soghoman Tehlerian. Before long he migrated to Fresno, California, where, in 1969, he died and was buried in the Ararat Cemetery. Above the grave rose a monument in memory of "the national hero, who, on March 15, 1921, brought justice upon Talaat Pasha, a principal perpetrator of the Armenian Genocide in 1915, which claimed the lives of 1,500,000 Armenian martyrs."[3]

Operation Nemesis took the lives of five of the seven Turkish culprits it had originally targeted for assassination. Enver Pasha, although targeted, escaped by way of Tiflis, thence to Moscow, where he met a woman no less adventuresome than he, Louise Bryant, widow of John Reed, and for a time went freebooting among the Bolsheviks. He died in battle against the Red Army in Turkestan in 1922. The notorious Dr. Nazim, a Pan-Turkish fanatic, also escaped his avengers. Curiously, he was executed by Mustafa Kemal in 1926 for plotting against the government. Kemal, who rose to power in the CUP, took no part in avenging or punishing those responsible for the great atrocity committed against the Armenians. On the contrary, his feelings on that point were not very different from those of Talaat, whose murder, he later said, "almost broke my heart."[4]

Private vengeance of the sort exacted by Operation Nemesis would have found less justification had "crimes against humanity" been part of international law codes during the First World War. The roots of the concept reached back to the First Hague Convention of 1899, wherein "the laws of humanity" and "the requirements of public conscience" were held to be part of the fabric of the law of nations. The judicial arm of the Paris Peace Conference, the Commission of Responsibilities and Sanctions, took cognizance of this earlier declaration in its review of "barbarous and illegitimate methods of warfare." Whether any sanction reached the crime against the Armenians was unclear. They, after all, were inhabitants of Turkey. But Nicholas Politus, the Greek member of the commission, believed that it did and actually won adoption, ex post facto, of this standard. The final report held the Central Powers, including Turkey, accountable for crimes against humanity. Nothing substantial came of the holding. One year later, however, the Sèvres Treaty promulgated by the Allies stipulated trial and punishment for Turkish transgressions and in Article 230 reserved the right of the signatories to designate an appropriate tribunal for trial. The treaty, alas, was aborted. Nevertheless, a leading student of our time, Vahakn Dadrian, attributes extraordinary significance to the Sèvres provisions. For the first time in history, he writes, deliberate mass murder was designated a crime in international law "to be adjudicated in accordance with domestic penal codes." At last, in 1949, the United Nations Convention on Genocide declared it "a code of domestic crimes, which are already denominated common law crimes."[5]

In the absence of any such provision in 1919, nothing resulted but occasional show trials under authority of the sovereign deemed responsible for these alleged crimes against humanity. This was the case in Germany, where Kaiser Wilhelm was the principal culprit. The trials took place in German courts under German rules, and of course were a fiasco, in the view of the Allies. The Sublime Porte, in order to appease the Allies, conducted a military trial of Talaat, Enver, and Djemal in absentia, and condemned them to death. While this sentence was without avail, lesser officials, not so fortunate as to have escaped, were tried in similar tribunals and publicly hanged in Hayasid Square, Stamboul. The first of the culprits to be executed, Kemal Bey, was said to be a particularly brutal underling.[6] With the rise of Mustafa Kemal and the omission of any punitive clauses in the Treaty of Lausanne, successor to Sèvres, in 1923, all such proceedings came to an end.

Lacking any public retribution for the crime against the Armenians, indeed any recognition by the perpetrator of their collective martyrdom, the crime festered in the hearts of the Armenian people until it became a hallmark of their national character.

A trial of a different sort tested the American humanitarian effort to help the Armenian victims. Near East Relief, having raised $51,361,804.92 since its inception, ended the year 1920 with a budgetary balance of over $4.5 million. Money poured into the New York office at the rate of $40,000 a day. By the beginning of the new year every state had its own volunteer committee and fund-raising was at an all-time high. Nevertheless, public resistance to giving to the relief of the "starving Armenians" was also on the rise, and there was talk of retrenchment at headquarters. The Greco-Turkish War, rising toward a climax in 1922, put an unexpected strain on the organization's resources, and a 25 percent cut in relief appropriations was proposed. In March Charles Vickrey, the general secretary, issued a special appeal: "Will America Commute the Death Sentence?" Fancying the American people as the jury in a case of impending disaster, Vickrey pleaded, "The 25 per cent cut literally means death to thousands upon thousands of innocent children. Death just as certainly as if those thousands of children were lined up along the Avenue and shot down with machine guns!" Commute the death sentence! he concluded.[7]

In April the *Literary Digest,* a widely read weekly, reiterated the plea in a full-page editorial, "Sentenced to Die," which also ran as an advertisement in the *New York Times* and other newspapers. It picked up the idea and theme of Vickrey's appeal. "In Armenia a Christian race is being blotted out—while the world looks on."

> Last year 140 villages were destroyed; thousands of mothers and grown daughters were violated and slain; fathers were herded into buildings and burned; multitudes of orphaned children were driven into the wilderness to wander and die,

unless, perchance, they might be gathered, like lost lambs, into folds of safety by the Near East Relief.

The editorial, with vivid details of hunger and suffering, ended with an invocation of the message of Easter: "*You* can speak the word of Resurrection which will call back some little child from the dark valley of shadows and flood its new life with sunshine." The Christian appeal, with a visual counterpart in the NER posters, worked. The cut was rescinded, the sentence suspended.[8]

The course of events in Turkey certainly offered no grounds for complacency in the offices of Near East Relief. The Armenian problem had become interlaced with the problem of another Christian minority, the Greeks. Although the European Greeks had won their independence from the Ottoman Empire in 1832, millions of the "unredeemed"—remnants of the Byzantine Empire—were scattered from the Aegean islands to Thrace and thence along the Pontus littoral of the Black Sea. The Treaty of Sèvres virtually invited the Greeks to revive the dream of Hellenic empire in Asia Minor. In his testimony at the Tehlerian trial in Berlin, Lepsius recalled what Count Metternich, the German ambassador in Constantinople in 1918, had written: "The Armenians are finished. The Young Turk gang is impatiently awaiting the moment when the Greeks will turn on Turkey. Hellenism is the cultural element of Turkey. It will be destroyed as the Armenian element was."[9] One of those Young Turks, Mustafa Kemal, having disposed of the Armenian problem in Cilicia, to the south, and secured the eastern border with Soviet Armenia, now turned his attention to the Greek menace.

Kemal's army had driven one and a half million Greeks from the Pontus, killing 360,000 in the process.[10] (The population of another and smaller Christian minority, the Assyrians, Nestorian in religion, was reduced by two-thirds.) Near East Relief, while its roots were Protestant, gave alms as well to Roman Catholics, Greek Orthodox, and Nestorians. Armenian Christians and the missionaries to them were sometimes caught up in Turkish campaigns against brethren of the faith. Marsovan, the seat of Anatolia College, in close proximity to Samsoun, on the Black Sea, was the scene of an ugly incident in 1921. The head Turkish-language instructor in the college, a Kurd, was killed near the compound; extensive searches were carried out; several teachers lost their lives. Finally, all the Americans, headed by the college's president, George E. White, were expelled, except two who looked after the children in the NER orphanage. Soon the women's college and the hospital were shut down. The disturbance arose from the belief of government officials that the Pontus Literary Society in the college was a subversive Hellenist organization. To pick up the account of Charles T. Riggs:

> In July, Osman Agha (Peg-leg) and his 'chetes' marched into the city for a week and burned, looted, and massacred without restraint. More than a thousand of the Christian population of the city (most of them women and children) succeeded in reaching the college before Osman put a guard around the walls and prevented more from coming.

After the college closed its doors, most of the Armenian and Greek inhabitants left Marsovan.[11]

The American high commissioner, Admiral Bristol, at Constantinople, acquiesced in the charge leveled by the Angora government that the Literary Society was a front for Greek propaganda. The Marsovan incident, combined with Bristol's nonresponse, underscored the new reality of Kemalist control of interior parts of Turkey. The provincial governors no longer listened to the dying regime in Constantinople. Authority, as Bristol repeatedly said, had passed to local officialdom, and it was under no restraints in dealing with NER or with Christian missionaries. While he may have been right about that, the admiral's failure to investigate or protest the killings and expulsions in Marsovan prompted James L. Barton to lay his objections before the State Department and to call for Bristol's removal on the grounds that his partiality for the Turks made him unfit for his office. The missionary leader had been at odds with the diplomat almost from the beginning of their relationship. The conflict was grounded, as Barton realized, in their different purposes, one seeking friendly relations with the powers that be, the other dedicated to humanitarian relief. Barton and William W. Peet, his colleague at Constantinople, had fidgeted at some length over the matter before Barton filed his complaint. The admiral, hearing of it from Washington, remarked breezily, "The missionaries are taking a crack at me." Barton, on seeing the department's response—a slap on the wrist—wrote to Peet, "It seemed to us here that it is on the whole a very meek affair." Both men continued to believe that Bristol, although a devoted, forthright, and honorable public servant, put commercial advantage before the best interests of his countrymen in the Near East.[12]

Another incident rising out of the hostility of the Angora government to Near East Relief took the name of "Yowell's Yowl." Major Forest D. Yowell, the NER field director at Harpoot in 1922, together with Dr. Mark Ward, director of the orphanage, and several other workers were forcibly expelled because of protests against the persecution of Christians, both Armenian and Greek. Frictions there had developed over a cloth-weaving contract employing Armenian orphans and led to seizure of buildings and other property owned or leased by NER. Yowell complained that he was "constantly badgered" by local officials. The sensational core of the conflict lay elsewhere, however. Yowell spelled it out in a letter to J. B. Jackson, the U.S. consul at Aleppo, on April 5, 1922.

> The Armenians in the Vilayet [Mamouret ul Aziz] are in a
> state of slavery. They are not permitted to leave the vilayet
> and N.E.R. was forced to refund to Headquarters about
> 75,000 banknotes received from Americans for travel expenses

[for Armenians] to leave the country. The properties of the heirs of Armenians killed in the deportations are taken by the Turks. . . . A recent Turkish law prevents any Christians from inheriting property except from a father or a brother; all properties left to other relatives go to the government. . . . Christian men and boys are thrown into jail for no reason whatever and made to pay large sums of money before they are released and Christian women are forced into the houses of Muslims as their slaves.

Yowell went on to speak of the deportation of the Black Sea Greeks, some of whom passed through Harpoot. "Along all the routes taken by the Greeks are the bodies of the dead which are being consumed by dogs, wolves, and vultures."[13]

Yowell's report leaked and produced screaming headlines in London on May 5, then immediately crossed the Atlantic. Herbert Adams Gibbons, now foreign correspondent of the *Christian Science Monitor,* pursued this story for several weeks in the spring. Mark Ward contributed a sensational article, "The Greatest Massacre in History," to the *New York Times.* Gibbons graphically described the assault on the Pontine Greeks all the way from Sinope to Trebizond. For Near East Relief Gibbons had nothing but praise. "It stands as a great constructive agency saving and instilling a spirit of hope and progress where all is darkness." For Bristol, of course, the story was but another instance of NER propaganda. The main effect was to poison the feelings of the Turks for the United States. At some point criticism of the emerging regime was likely to become counterproductive. One of Yowell's fellow workers, Mary Caroline Holmes, the director at Urfa, wrote Bristol that the accusation "not only jeopardized N.E.R. activities in 'Kemalistan' but missionary work as well." A much-traveled relief worker, Florence Billings, protégé of the venerated Annie Allen, publicly declared that the Yowell-Ward indictment was untrue, though she had no firsthand knowledge of events at Harpoot. Billings had accompanied Allen upon her appointment as NER's representative in Angora. There her sympathies went over to the nationalists. At the invitation of the government she and Allen inspected and reported on the villages ravaged and burned by the Greeks to the east of Angora. NER headquarters looked askance upon the publicity given to its personnel. Nevertheless, "Yowell's Yowl" created a great commotion among Armenia's American friends, who bombarded Congress and the State Department with demands for action.[14]

Reports of the new atrocities also stirred the British conscience. Late in May A. C. Geddes, His Majesty's ambassador to the United States, called the attention of Secretary of State Charles Evans Hughes to the revival by the Angora Turks of the deportation and massacre of Christian minorities, and asked the United States to join the European Allies in an investigation. Hughes at once raised the question of American participation in this effort with President Warren G. Harding. Bristol, having learned of Whitehall's diplomatic initiative from the British high commissioner at Constantinople, promptly cabled his objections to Washington. Always suspicious of the British, he thought they were seizing upon these alarmist reports from Anatolia to whip up anti-Turkish propaganda. Undersecretary Allen Dulles inclined to agree. Harding, after reviewing the British request, said it would be difficult to withhold our participation in a matter so deeply interesting to the American people. He had already felt the lash of the Armenian lobby and wanted no more of it. Yet the United States, he told Hughes, was utterly helpless to do anything. "I am wondering," he moaned, "if the possible manifestation of our impotence would be more humiliating than our own non-participation is distressing." And with this he left the issue to the secretary's judgment. John Finley penned a timely editorial in the *New York Times,* headed "R.S.V.P.," in which he maintained that American participation in the inquiry was morally obligatory if, once again, "great expectations" were not to be answered with "great refusals." Hughes, perhaps thinking to return to the good graces of the Armenophiles, chose to accept the invitation. Meanwhile, Geddes told of new outrages. "It would naturally be said," Hughes wrote to the president of his decision to comply, "that we were far more solicitous about American interest in oil than about Christian lives." Besides, American presence in the inquiry would be a moderating influence. Near East Relief, of course, would welcome American involvement, as Barton had signaled to Hughes; but it mattered scarcely at all to the American Board of Foreign Missions, whose chairmanship was the second hat Barton wore. By this time the last missionary had already left the Eastern Turkish Mission, and the corps was much depleted in central Turkey. As events unfolded, France, having earlier made its separate peace with the Angora government, deflected the British overture with the suggestion that a neutral agency—the International Red Cross, for instance—be asked to investigate the alleged massacres. The IRC gingerly took up the charge without conclusive result.[15]

On August 26, 1922, Mustafa Kemal commenced his march to the Aegean, crushing and decimating the Greek enemy all the way to Smyrna, the second city of Turkey—ancient Ionia, today Izmir—and its major seaport, restored to Greece in 1920 with an extensive hinterland for five years, after which its future, whether Greek or Turkish, would be determined by plebiscite. Many Armenians, refugees from Cilicia for the most part, had crowded into Smyrna. The city's normal population of 350,000 had been doubled by the influx of refugees. Behind the long waterfront, lined with warehouses and richly complemented villas, lay the ethnic quarters of the city, the Greeks and the Armenians on one side, the Turks on the other. There was a small American colony: NER and YMCA workers, consular staff, teachers in the American college, and others engaged in the commerce of the port.[16]

Kemal's army entered the city on September 9. The Greek army, soundly whipped, had already fled. On the 13th a great fire ravaged the city and burned for days, consuming everything in its path. "What a hellish scene!" wrote one eyewitness, Abraham H. Hartunian, a refugee from Marash who had gone to Smyrna in quest of American visas for himself and his family. "The quay was bulging with humanity from end to end. Exhausted! Defeated! Pale! Terrified! Hopeless. The sea on one side, the flames on the other."[17] The cause of the conflagration was never definitely established. But American observers, almost without exception, said the torch was lit by Turkish soldiers in the Armenian quarter. John Clayton, a *Chicago Tribune* reporter, wrote, "Except for the squalid Turkish quarter, Smyrna has ceased to exist. The problem of the minorities is here solved for all time. No doubt remains as to the origin of the fire. . . . The torch was applied by Turkish regular soldiers."[18] Viewed in the context of the whole tragic epoch, the death toll from fire and slaughter in Smyrna scarcely mattered. The American consul, George Horton, placed it at 100,000; Admiral Bristol, always careful not to "blackguard the Turk," said the dead did not exceed 2,000. For Horton, with Esther Lovejoy and others, the bloody scene completed the long twisting whirl of disaster. Dr. Lovejoy called it "the spectacular finale." Horton only embroidered her language when he wrote, "Smyrna was a fittingly lurid and Satanic finale to the whole dreadful tragedy."[19]

In her memoir, *Certain Samaritans,* Lovejoy recalled the scene when she arrived in the harbor on a tramp steamer for duty in the unprecedented emergency. "There were approximately 300,000 people huddled together on the cobblestones of the Smyrna waterfront and hiding in the ruins. . . . For ten days and nights, they had held their places." They desperately hoped for rescue by sea. U.S. destroyers in the harbor offered assistance to American citizens only. Some Greek merchant ships and an Italian ocean liner carried many others to safety. It was not nearly enough. In this crisis forty-five-year-old Asa Jennings, an American YMCA worker, stepped into the role of hero in what might have been a Gilbert and Sulli-

Dynamiting the walls of buildings along the quay during the fire at Smyrna

van operetta were it not so serious. All else failing, he sent a wireless to Athens pleading for twenty ships and signed his name. Who was Asa Jennings? the wireless responded. After some straight talk, in which Jennings confessed to incompetence in maritime matters, Athens agreed to place all ships afloat in the Aegean under command of "Admiral" Jennings for emergency removal of refugees from Smyrna. At midnight, September 23, he ran up the American flag and led a flotilla packed with 15,000 refugees to the nearest Greek island, Mytilene. The fleet returned for more, and by the time the operation was completed some 200,000 had been evacuated. Perhaps as many as half were Armenian.[20] To a significant degree, the Armenian problem had been removed from Turkey to Greece.

Yet another finale—this one of international diplomacy—awaited. At Lausanne, on the Lake of Geneva, a conference opened in the fall of 1922 to draft a treaty to replace the discarded Treaty of Sèvres and thus, finally, to make peace between the Allies and Turkey. Meanwhile, Kemal proclaimed the abolition of the sultanate and the exile of the sultan and his family, preparing the way for his own ascendancy as president of the new Turkey. The United States, retaining its observer status, was represented at Lausanne by Richard Washburn Child, ambassador to Italy and head of the Special Mission; Joseph C. Grew, an experienced Foreign Service officer, currently U.S. minister to Switzerland; and Admiral Bristol. Barton and Peet, with credentials from the Federal Council of Churches, were on hand throughout. Secretary of State Hughes had prepared an aide-mémoire, to which Barton had contributed, outlining the American position on the critical issues that would come before the conference. First, retention of capitulations as far as they were essential to the protection of American rights and interests. Second, the reopening and safeguarding of American educational and philanthropic institutions. Third, freedom of the straits. Fourth, an "open door" to American commerce. Fifth, indemnification for loss of American lives and property since 1914. Sixth, guarantees for the protection of religious minorities, including provision of an Armenian homeland. And still other points respecting foreign debts and access to archaeological sites.[21] Lord Curzon, the British foreign secretary, an erudite and accomplished diplomat whom the Americans found wily and overbearing, presided at the conference. Child said Curzon was "pompous and puffing" and took a dim view of his maneuvers on behalf of British power and commerce, particularly claims on Mesopotamian oil.[22] Suspicion and jealousy between the British and the French undercut the Allied position in the negotiations and strengthened the hand of the Turks, led by Ismet Pasha, basking in the nationalist victory over the Greeks. The conference passed through two stages. It broke up in February 1923 when Curzon and Ismet could not agree on a draft treaty, but resumed on April 23 and finished its work three months later.

Armenians were no more than kibitzers around the table at Lausanne. Their hopes and interests were scarcely mentioned, much less discussed, by the treaty makers. The Turkish delegation threw up a stone wall before the issue of protection of minorities. On January 6 Riza Nour Bey, the number two man in the delegation, created a scandal by walking out of the subcommittee on minorities when the question of an Armenian homeland was broached. In a front-page story in the *New York Times* Edwin L. James wrote that Riza Nour denounced the Allies for using the Armenians to incite the Turks and thereby bringing about their own ruin. He refused to listen to Armenian plaints and projects and marched out with his aide close behind. Three days later James reported that Ismet reiterated his pledge that the minorities would have the same rights as other Turkish citizens, in accord with the principle the Allies had written into treaties with several Balkan nations. Curzon, thinking the pledge hollow, deplored Turkish obstinacy in this matter but would not jeopardize the conference and agreement on other important issues, chiefly commercial and financial. Ismet drew a parallel between a home in Georgia or Mississippi for African-Americans and an Armenian homeland in Turkey. Child remarked, "The Negro is a problem—so is the Armenian. The Negro has been lynched and mobbed. So has the Armenian. The only difference is the Armenian was found on Turkish soil, while we actually imported the Negro against his will." A better American example, he supposed, might be the reservations created for the Indians, though that was hardly "a happy experiment." Barton and Peet prepared a special memorandum on the homeland, thinking it the only solution to the twin problem of orphans and refugees regardless of other considerations. Basically what had for so long been treated as a matter of protecting Christian minorities was transmuted into a refugee problem. George R. Montgomery, on behalf of the American Armenia Society, authored another homeland memorial. Ismet would not budge. President Harding, in Washington, told Hughes it was all very discouraging, "but I frankly do not see how we can do more than strongly appeal in their [the Armenians'] behalf." The employment of armed force was out of the question.[23]

As the second phase of the conference opened in April, according to Grew, the corridors buzzed with news that the Angora government had revived the long-dormant Chester Concession, originally conferred on the American rear admiral Colby M. Chester in 1909 for development of railroads, oil, and other resources in the eastern Ottoman Empire, from which both countries might benefit. It had failed for want of capital. It was still poor, but with the encouragement of the State Department, the Chester Concession was put in play again. "Each village," an American missionary wrote, "seems to feel that wealth . . . is going to pour in from rich American investors." But the rocket fell like the proverbial stick; the Angora parliament annulled the concession before the year was out. Oil was not a mirage in the Near East, however. Standard Oil of New Jersey, at the head of the Rockefeller empire, was already on the scene, and it persuaded the State Department to break the stranglehold the Anglo-Persian Oil Company had on the rich resources of Mesopotamia. The mastermind of this business, "the Talleyrand of oil diplomacy," not surprisingly, was an Armenian, Calouste Sarkis Gulbenkian, and he finally got the British to let the Americans into the game.[24]

No Armenian homeland, no protection for Christian minorities, no capitulations or guarantees of American institutions, no indemnities or recognition of American claims—obviously the treaty was a defeat for the United States as well as for the Armenians. "In the treaty of Lausanne," Winston Churchill remarked, "history will search in vain for the word 'Armenia.'" For that land and people it was the ultimate betrayal. For Henry Morgenthau, who had been "present at the creation," as it were, the treaty was the consummation of "Allied greed." Lord Curzon found more sorrow than pride in his work. "Oil weighed more than Armenian blood," he repined. The retrospection of historians, at least in the West, has not altered the verdict. And the French scholar Yves Ternon has captured the moral horror of it all: "The crime is dictated by imperious interests, reasoned, often carefully weighed, always economic, sometime ideological, rarely religious. Between those who conceive of it and those who would prevent it, there are too many golden handshakes and rivers of oil: the simplest humanitarianism is not up to the task."[25] That assessment has the sagacity of Joseph Conrad.

As the conference wound down, Ismet and Grew had their private pourparler to draw up a treaty of comity and commerce between their two countries. This arrangement, of course, was planned and authorized by the State Department. The terms of the agreement were to be consistent with the Allied-Turkish treaty. The final pact, while below Grew's expectations, was sent to Washington in August 1923. Over three years would pass, however, before the accord was sent to the U.S. Senate for ratification. Meanwhile, Barton and Peet, the former at Congregational House in Boston, the latter at Bible House in Constantinople, continued to wrestle with the intertwined problems of the American Board and Near East Relief. They refused to be discouraged. Peet said that the most important incident of the conference occurred not at the negotiating table but in off-the-record conversations with Turkish delegates and their aides, who expressed appreciation and offered assurance for the continuation of American educational, religious, and philanthropic work in the country. To be sure, these were not written guarantees; yet they seemed to have been given in earnest. Bristol, too, suddenly seemed sympathetic. So Barton concluded his report on the Lausanne Conference on a forward-looking note.

"Our recourse is therefore not to a rediscussion of the past and the injustice to the Christians . . . but to look to the future." It was, indeed, "to make the most of the situation."[26]

From Greece, Dr. Esther Lovejoy, among the last Americans to leave the smoldering harbor of Smyrna at the end of September 1922, later telegraphed an American friend:

> Refugee conditions indescribable. People, mostly women and children. Rejected by all the world. Unable to speak Greek language. Herded and driven like animals from place to place. Crowded into damp holes and hovels. Wet, cold, hungry, sick; suffering very great. Mercy of immediate death withheld. Greece willing but utterly unable to cope with conditions. Outlook here hopeless. Help from America only hope.

The dispatch was read into the *Congressional Record*.[27] The conflagration with its 200,000 or more refugees was a terrible setback to Near East Relief after it had weathered the funding crisis earlier in the year.

Armenian refugees, sprinkled through the Aegean islands, fanned out from Macedonia through the Peloponnesus. Hunger and disease were rampant among the 10,000 children under the care of Dr. Mabel Elliott, formerly of the Caucasus, for Near East Relief in association with American Women's Hospitals. Some were billeted in pretty fancy places—the Zappeian Exposition Hall and the former Royal Palace in Athens, also the deposed Kaiser's summer palace in Corfu. In the emergency all of NER's rules against extending care to adults, particularly men, broke down. The Greek government, once again under the commoner Venizelos, breaking under the weight of its generosity, turned to the League of Nations to expedite the resettlement of refugees. The League set up the Refugee Settlement Commission, consisting of four members. Henry Morgenthau, the commission's chairman, went to Athens

The trek from Harpoot to the Levant

in 1923, just ten years after he became U.S. ambassador at Constantinople. Quite aside from this commission, the League undertook the responsibility of carrying out the special convention on population exchange between Greece and Turkey entered into at Lausanne. It was the first large compulsory population exchange in history. Approximately 345,000 Turks in Macedonia, identified as Muslims, were exchanged for 150,000 Greeks, identified as Christians, in Turkey and eastern Thrace. Although the numbers favored the Turks, it was commonly said that, measured by education and skills, the exchange favored the Greeks. It was, at any rate, a remarkable commentary on Wilsonian "self-determination of nations." It defused an explosive ethnic conflict between Greece and Turkey, and so was politically astute; yet, in the judgment of some observers, it too readily bowed to the proposition that peoples of different nationalities and religions could not live together in peace.[28]

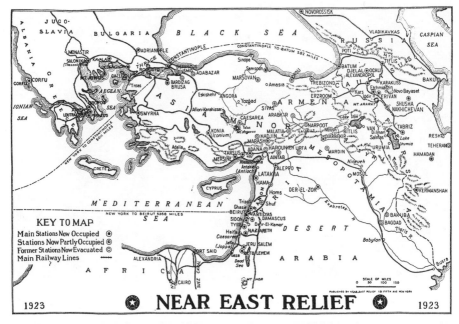

Near East Relief map, 1923

Fridtjof Nansen, the Norwegian explorer, savant, and human-itarian—recipient of the Nobel Peace Prize in 1922 for his work with Russian refugees—is generally credited with the idea of the Greek-Turkish population exchange. As the League's high commissioner for refugees, he also originated the "Nansen passport," which has been well described as "a title to existence" for stateless persons. According to the League, some 300,000 Armenian refugees were without valid papers. And then there were the Greeks, the Assyrians, the Russians, all Christians, as well as the Jews. They were scattered through the Near East, the largest number being in mainland Greece and Syria. The Nansen passports regularized their status as refugees. Near East Relief still had plenty to do. In 1923, with an overseas staff numbering 225, it operated 124 orphanages with 64,000 children. The Protestant missionary face of the organization was rapidly withering. Admiral Bristol, one imagines with a chuckle in his throat, remarked on the disappearance of the missionaries' clientele: "It can safely be assumed that by the end of the year not a single Armenian will be left in Anatolia. . . . We shall then witness a real, true Turkey for the Turks."[29]

The Armenian Soviet Republic figured prominently in Nansen's work under the League. In 1924 the Greek government, its patience running out along with its resources, felt the urgent necessity to evict 50,000 Armenians. Nansen, in response, came up with a plan to resettle many of the refugees in the cotton-growing lands of the Araxes Valley, below Mount Ararat. Progress was proceeding apace in Bolshevik Armenia. "The rapid return to approximate normalcy during the last three years is almost unbelievable," Ernest Yarrow wrote near the end of 1924. The Polygon orphanage—"nation of orphans"—in Alexandropol, now Leninakan, was still a marvel, though its population had shrunk to 11,000 in 1925. Agricultural improvement had been impressive, even when it resembled an American Wild West show. Settlers instinctively circled their wagons to protect the livestock from roving banditti. The NER's Paul H. Phillips, superintendent of the model ranch at Karra Kalla, told of a fight with Tartar cattle rustlers. Surrounded, outnumbered, his wife beaten, Phillips dispatched an orphan worker on horseback for help. The family was rescued but not before the outlaws had ransacked the house and driven off the cattle.[30]

Nansen, as noted, proposed to relocate the refugees on the desert-like plain of the Araxes west of Erivan. His travel journal of the venture was published in 1928 under the title *Armenia and the Near East*. The Norwegian stopped in Constantinople, where a remnant of 5,000 Armenian refugees remained. He visited St. Sophia, the domed masterpiece of Byzantine church architecture, observing keenly:

> It is remarkable that the creative idea [the lofty dome] of St. Sophia at Byzantium and of St. Peter's at Rome, the two

greatest cathedrals of the Roman churches of the East and the West, should have originated in the Armenian mind, in the heretical Gregorian Church, with its despised Monophysite teaching that Christ had one nature only, the divine, and yet became perfect Man.[31]

Nansen, it seems safe to say, was unacquainted with the country of Armenia until his brush with Greece; but he was emotionally drawn to it, both for its rich cultural tradition and because it had suffered more and survived more than any other nation in the Great War. He heaped praise on Near East Relief, and thought that the independent Armenian Republic's submission to the Soviet Union was "doubtless inevitable." His ambitious project required extensive acquisition, reclamation, and settlement of undeveloped land. Largely on the promise of it, some 4,000 Armenian refugees, most of them from Greece, resettled in this "homeland" in 1926.[32] Sad to say, it was a colossal failure. Although the Soviet government was supportive, the League of Nations lacked funds to finance the project and a privately floated loan was unsuccessful. Turning away in disgust, Nansen linked his disappointment to the "grim tale of broken and unfulfilled promises" that marked the history of the Armenian people. "Woe to the Armenians, that they were ever drawn into European politics!" Nansen declared. "It would have been better for them if the name of Armenia had never been uttered by any European diplomatist."[33]

Nansen's project represented, as his biographer has said, his own personal crusade; it did not depend on the League of Nations or, for that matter, Near East Relief, which was rapidly phasing out its work in the Caucasus when that project began. As early as the fall of 1922, NER had begun the difficult work of transporting orphans from places like Harpoot and Sivas in eastern Anatolia to the more hospitable environs of Syria in the Levant. The safety of the orphans and of those who looked after them could no longer be as-

Armenian refugees at Beirut

sured in Kemalist Turkey. *New Near East* carried a two-page photographic spread on the arduous 500-mile trek of 5,000 children to their new quarters. In long caravans they alternately walked and mounted camels and donkeys through the mountainous and desert country.[34] NER's annual report for 1923 said that more than 22,000 orphans had been transported to the Mediterranean littoral extending from Beirut to Jerusalem, and more would follow. The orphan count of the Polygon had fallen to 9,000 by the time an earthquake struck Leninakan in 1926. In that year, when Yarrow went home, the remaining orphans came under Soviet Armenian care.

The showplace of the new orphan colony was the Bird's Nest, under Maria Jacobsen, on the ancient Phoenician coast at Sidon. France was the mandatory power in these lands, and mandatory funds as well as funds from the Nansen office helped NER construct crude "urban settlements" for the children. Peet and Vickrey made a visit to inspect the orphanage, as well as a nearby refugee camp, in 1924. They found a spread-out, somewhat disheveled

Maria Jacobsen at the Bird's Nest orphanage at Sidon

village of huts on a sun-baked beach. The orphans and refugees busied themselves with industry suited to their skills and seemed healthy and happy. Henry H. Riggs, knowing the disappointment and distress that had led them to this place, took a grim view of it. "The crowds of American and European tourists leave their luxurious steamers and follow perhaps a morbid curiosity to see in a great camp poverty and squalor and misery and suffering carried to the nth degree." The camp of some 200 acres sheltered 12,000, and rows of shops and tables invited the trade of tourists.[35]

Back home NER struggled with the deepening deficit into which the Smyrna disaster had plunged it. In 1923 the executive committee of the board of trustees brought in Henry J. Allen, who had just completed a term as governor of Kansas, to survey current operations and make cost-cutting recommendations. He saw no prospects for the organization in Anatolia. The new government under Kemal regarded NER's officers and workers as enemies. Peet was saddened by the turn of events. Good work was still being done and it would be to "our everlasting shame," he declared, to leave it unfinished. He, more than anyone else, however, knew that the Americans were unwanted. As the overseas director of American Board missions, he had seen them all but disappear; and, of course, this threw a shadow over his work for NER. The verbal promises made by the Turkish negotiators at Lausanne with regard to so-called American institutions proved worthless. Schools and colleges, no longer privileged, found it hard to continue. Many closed. Peet was shocked by the cessation of Marash College and the hospital there, despite assurances to the contrary. Barton, disheartened by the closure of Euphrates College, over which he had once presided, sought in vain to transfer it to Erivan. A problem particularly annoying to Peet was the new requirement that American physicians must take a course or courses in a Turkish medical school to obtain a license to practice. Harassment on this order was intolerable.[36]

Although retrenchment was the order of the day, Near East Relief still had a million contributors annually, many thriving state and regional chapters, and even a new international program with active chapters in fourteen countries. An offshoot of this endeavor was the organization of NER's first international conference, in Geneva, in 1924. It led the following year to the first Golden Rule Sunday in the same city. This was Vickrey's brainchild. The well-laid banquet had as its menu a four-cent meal, the equivalent of the food served daily at NER orphanages. The guests, after this meager repast, were invited to make an appropriate donation. The Christian Golden Rule was thus affirmed. The *Rochester Democrat,* commenting on the event, said that thinking people should not need to be reminded of a rule of conduct so elemental, yet the world is full of evidence to the contrary, and the genius of the occasion was to call this rule dramatically to memory.[37] For the next seven years Golden Rule Sunday was a regular event on the philanthropy's calendar at home and abroad. Henry J. Allen called it NER's "greatest asset."

Turning its back on Turkey, NER transferred its overseas headquarters from Constantinople to Athens. As things wound down, Henry H. Riggs, representing the third generation of his family in Anatolia, was moved to write of the disappearance of "the visible fruits of a century of intensive missionary work." All through Turkey, with some exception for Constantinople, "ruined churches and empty schools stand as mute reminders of the missionary past." And in the press the evangels were described as "lost people wandering amid the wreckage of their lives." It was time to go home. The imperturbable Peet left in 1925 after forty years' service in Turkey. His erstwhile adversary, Admiral Bristol, returned to the United States about the same time with high praise for the new regime in Turkey. Henry Morgenthau had just completed a round-the-world tour. Cleveland Dodge, the long-time tight-lipped treasurer of the organization, died in 1926. The president, James L. Bar-

Children of the Zappeion orphanage in Athens at play in the temple of Zeus

Near East Relief poster, 1926

ton, would turn his incredible energies to writing a book, *Story of Near East Relief* (1930). In this undertaking he may have been reminded of the prophetic inscription on an old Assyrian tablet, conjecturally dated 2800 B.C., hidden in a dark corner of a museum in Constantinople, of which he and Peet had been apprised at Lausanne. According to a translation got from Isabel Dodd, it read: "Our earth is degenerate in these latter days. There are signs that the world is speedily coming to an end. Children no longer obey their parents. Every man wants to write a book. The end of the world is evidently approaching."[38]

In keeping with its usual policy, Near East Relief took no official position on the draft treaty of friendship and commerce between the United States and Turkey. The perception was that most of the organization's leaders opposed it. James L. Barton, however, was conspicuous in his support for it. Peet noticed with some surprise that in a *Literary Digest* symposium on the treaty, after the text was released in the fall of 1923, Barton was the only panelist who favored its ratification.[39] Peet himself finally endorsed the treaty. Both were following the path of accommodation with Turkey earlier marked out by Caleb Gates, president of Robert College and Admiral Bristol's quondam golfing partner. Interviewed for an article in *The Congregationalist*—an article that never appeared—Barton was quoted as saying, "We have all the oral promises we need to continue this work; the test will come in performance. We are proposing to test it out." He maintained this posture despite accumulating evidence of negative results. A valued Armenian Board missionary, Reverend Ralph S. Harlow, long in service at Smyrna International College, vigorously opposed this stance in *Outlook* and elsewhere and was forced to resign from the college. The American Board, he argued, "ought to have stood four square against the wretched treaty."[40]

The American Committee for the Independence of Armenia (ACIA) launched a campaign against ratification of the treaty, which it viewed as part and parcel of the heinous Allied accord at Lausanne. On November 25, 1923, at New York's Yale Club, a battery of dignitaries led by Oscar Straus, the former ambassador to Turkey, denounced the treaty. It was "diabolically one-sided," he said, giving everything to Turkey, nothing to the United States and Armenia. Before long James W. Gerard, Rabbi Stephen Wise, and others were on the hustings against the treaty. Repeatedly singled out for criticism was the failure of either treaty to protect the rights of Christian minorities. A glaring omission, one that was even embarrassing to Joseph Grew, concerned the right of Turkish-born naturalized citizens of the United States to visit Turkey without molestation. This was an insult to Armenian Americans. Tapping into the disgrace of American and Allied failure to secure the freedom and independence of Armenia, Gerard and other adversaries sought to shame the Senate into rejection of the treaty.[41] ACIA was joined in the campaign by the American Committee Opposed to the Lausanne Treaty, headed by David Hunter Miller, the prominent Wilsonian internationalist. Just back from his travels, Morgenthau jumped into the fray. He called Kemal "a brutal monster" who held tens of thousands of Armenian women in slavery. Approval of the treaty would dishonor the United States. "It is a purposeless and humiliating surrender to a red-handed faithless military despot." Edward Hale Bierstadt, in a hard-hitting book, *The Great Betrayal* (1924), wrote, "That treaty was signed in oil and sealed with the blood of the Greeks and Armenians."[42] Standard Oil was singled out as a powerful lobbyist for the treaty; and the infamous Chester Concession was pummeled to death, or would have been were it not already dead. The Democratic national platform in 1924 declared the party's opposition to the treaty; and a corps of Democratic senators led by William H. King of Utah lined up to defeat ratification.

Weighing the odds, President Calvin Coolidge at first withheld the treaty. Secretary of State Hughes put the administration on record in its support, however. In a speech before New York's Council on Foreign Relations in 1924, he recalled the history of American aloofness from Turkish affairs. If ever there was a time when we might have intervened to some purpose, it was in 1919, when we had troops abroad and were pressed to assume a mandate over Armenia or Turkey or both together. "But the opportunity passed," the secretary observed laconically. He rejected charges of oil diplomacy. Concluding, he said that if any Americans were qualified to speak for or against the treaty, they were Barton and Gates. And he read Barton's letter to him asserting that the treaty was the best that could be had under the circumstances, that the circumstances called for an agreement, and that the overwhelming sentiment of the American Board was that it should be ratified. He said nothing of the sentiments of Near East Relief.[43] The principal lobby for ratification of the treaty was the Council on Turkey-American Relations, chaired by George A. Plimpton. It made much of the new Turkey under Kemal, of the abolition of the sultanate and the caliphate, of liberal reforms, even the disappearance of the fez, and the peace and harmony that now reigned in that land, however deplorable were some of the means employed to attain power. Assuming the treaty was in the national interest, Grew, now at the State Department, may have put his finger on the hard moral issue facing the opponents: "Are we going to permit our righteous indignation over past injuries to exclude us effectively from opportunities to extend future help?"[44]

Finally, in the winter of 1926–27, the Turkish treaty was laid before the Senate, and after prolonged debate was rejected, January 18, on a vote of 50 for, 34 against —6 votes short of the requisite two-thirds majority. Howland Shaw, head of the Near East desk in the State Department, observed that American religious and educational philanthropies thus overshadowed the nation's commercial interests in Turkey.[45] The opposition took what gratification it could in this defeat. It was short-lived. Given a second chance, the treaty was ratified in 1929. Coincidentally, this was the year Near East Relief went out of business.

An organization "launched on a heart throb," as it was sometimes said, ended in heartbreak. Not that it had failed. It had, after all, over fifteen years raised approximately $100 million—say $3 billion in today's money—with untold amounts of in-kind donations for the relief of suffering in the Near East and contributed vitally to the survival of the Armenian people. Of this achievement the popular author Rose Wilder Lane wrote, "The world's history has never before recorded such a movement as this reaching out of sympathy—of charity, which is love—from the masses of us to the masses of other peoples whom we have not seen."[46] The accomplishment was all the more amazing because of the altruism that inspired and sustained it for fifteen years.

Yet Near East Relief had failed to attain an enduring place for the Armenian people in their Anatolian homeland despite the promises of the victorious powers in the Great War. The moral imperatives that drove NER somehow could not be aligned with the realpolitik of nations fighting over the spoils of war. Forces of history—nationalism, imperialism, capitalism, communism—and the rush of events overturned the best intentions of statesmen and diplomats. Humanitarianism did not stand a chance unless it was stiffened by the iron rod of national interest. Lacking that, NER was like the mythological Sisyphus, condemned to push its great stone up an insurmountable mountain.

As far back as 1924 Barton and his colleagues at NER had appointed what was called the Conservation Committee with a view to passing the responsibility for relief and reconstruction in their part of the world to other hands. There were assets to be cared for and, of course, the continuing need for aid and assistance. On July 1, 1929, the corporation had on hand $1 million in cash and pledges. Apparently a large ruble balance, with other assets, in the Caucasus was a dead loss. Worse, though it could not be publicly reported, thirty NER personnel had recently been arrested and either four or six of them shot. Immediate withdrawal from that dangerous quarter of the world was the only option.[47]

Meanwhile, at the instigation of Barclay Acheson, NER's director general, a comprehensive independent survey of needs and opportunities in most of the lands serviced by NER was undertaken in 1924. The resulting report, totally secular in spirit, was discussed at a conference in Constantinople, chaired by Bayard Dodge, in 1926. Finally, a 300-page book, *The Near East And American Philanthropy*, edited by Frank A. Ross and others, appeared in 1929. Basically, the survey paved the way for the transition from humanitarian relief to technical assistance and economic development. To implement this vision the Near East Foundation was incorporated in New York as the successor organization to Near East Relief. In the years since then it has carried out many educational and extension projects, chiefly in rural areas of the Near East. Of course, barring the Caucasus, very few Armenians are left in that part of the world to receive its aid.[48]

Epilogue: An Armenian American Chronicle

THE PITIABLE REMNANT OF Armenians beyond the borders of the tiny Caucasian appendage of the Soviet Union scattered in a diaspora across the face of the earth. In this exodus the United States of America was the favored destination. After all, but for America the Armenians might have ceased to exist. Reaching America's "golden door" was a struggle that called up all the strength and ingenuity and perseverance of the broken and battered nation.

Consider the odyssey of Haig Mnatzaganian, a fifteen-year-old beggar taken into the Near East Relief orphanage in Erivan. There he was encouraged to pursue his dream of an American life and education. Finding his way to Constantinople in 1921, Haig got a job with the British Allied Police under the occupation and studied at night at the YMCA. Of course, Haig kept in touch with NER. He saved enough money to take him to Greece—the second lap of his journey. At Piraeus he boarded a ship to Marseilles as a mess boy. From that port he made his way to Paris and found menial employment with the American legation. Again, after saving a few francs, Haig traveled to Le Havre and sought work on a steamer bound for America. He was told he had to have $50 to gain entrance; moreover, he ought to have someone on the other side to vouch for him. So he wrote to NER in New York. After some months, Haig, having saved $100, shipped on a steamer bound not to New York but to San Francisco. There, after a year's travail, an NER official met him at the gangplank; and Haig found employment and resumed his studies at the city's YMCA.[1]

Most immigrants, unlike Haig, passed through Ellis Island, in New York Harbor, but whatever their port of entry, they faced the restrictions of the immigration laws. The laws excluded illiterate adults, paupers, epileptics, and the victims of tuberculosis and loathsome or contagious diseases. Among Armenians trachoma was often a barrier to entry. The greatest barrier of all, however, was nationality or the absence of proof of it.

In 1920, according to official report, 10,212 Armenians were admitted to the United States, the largest tally on record. At this time Congress was about to reduce sharply the number of emigrants from eastern and southern Europe, the Near East, Asia, and other areas lightly represented in the current population of the United States. The stopgap National Quota Act of 1920 limited entrance yearly to 3 percent of the national group living in the United States in 1910. The rule obviously tilted toward the older Western European immigration and discouraged the so-called new immigration. The New Quota Law of 1924 further reduced the annual immigrant total from a given country to 2 percent of the national group in the population recorded in the census of 1890. This restriction cut the number of Armenians admitted to approximately 100 a year, or 0.03 percent by ethnic classification. Greeks, Turks, and other nationalities in their part of the world were similarly affected, though not to the same degree as the Armenians. Without recognized statehood, without recognized borders, the Armenians were also without a national quota. This lowered their demographic visibility. For a brief time they were charged to the Turkish quota, thereafter to the Soviet Union's. Friends of Armenia in Congress sought to amend the law to allow emergency admission of Armenian orphans and refugees, but without success. Of course, some immigrants were admitted regardless of quota: children of citizens, returning alien residents, and ministers and professors, for instance.[2]

But for the reactionary change of American immigration law after the World War, barring entrance to many of the "homeless, tempest-tossed" masses of whom Emma Lazarus sang, thousands upon thousands of Armenians would surely have come to the United States. All the compelling ingredients were there. The Armenians had need for refuge; they were largely literate, as well as skillful, tough, and tenacious; they were strongly drawn to America. With only the shred of a country to return to, and that under an alien regime, they were almost certain to become permanent residents, then citizens, adding their unique gifts to the variegated fabric of American life and culture. The Armenian community, about 100,000 in 1920, grew from within, for they prospered in their adopted country. Fortunately, after half a century, the quota system was repealed. Armenian immigrants then came in greater numbers—some 2,000 each year in the latter decades of the century. At its close the community numbered, as far as can be estimated, about 800,000.

Like other immigrant groups, the Armenians sought to recreate and preserve elements of their traditional culture while at the same time adapting and assimilating to the American fabric. They established fraternal societies and benevolent associations. They started special schools (*hai throts*) to keep alive the national language and customs, while other schools taught English and prepared the immigrant generation for naturalization. They established an Armenian-language newspaper. *The Hairenik,* originally in New York, then in Boston, was the first Armenian daily in the United States. In 1933 it added a weekly supplement in English. *Hairenik* was the organ of the Armenian Revolutionary Federation, or Dashnak party. The Armenians had become one of the most politicized people anywhere. The opposition Hunchaks split apart in the diaspora. Many of them entered the Ramgavar party, which, while more conservative than its rival, was paradoxically pro-Soviet in its outlook. Between the major parties no issue loomed larger in the American diaspora than their stance toward the Soviet regime in Armenia, the Dashnaks being aggressively hostile, the Ramgavars tending toward accommodation. The tug between rapid assimilation, on the one hand, and cleaving to the old ways, on the other hand, was characteristically most severe in the first generation. "How does it feel?" a new Armenian American was asked in the 1920s. He replied that "our cry of pain was not understood." He was reminded of a cartoon in a magazine showing a fat congressman, handkerchief to his eyes, exclaiming to pleading constituents, "Get out! You are breaking my heart." People turn away from suffering. There is too much brightness in America; it cannot face the dark.[3]

No institution was more important to the unity and identity of these new Americans than the Armenian Apostolic Church. In the opinion of some clerics, the church subordinated its spiritual mission to the preservation of Armenian nationality. In 1928 a young priest, Tiran Nersoyan, afterward primate of the Diocese of the Armenian Church in America, wrote an influential essay, "Nationalism or Gospel," admonishing believers against the secular error of "accented nationalism." The trauma of the genocide had caused Armenians to turn the church into an instrument of national survival. The issue thus formulated became a continuing theme in the history of the church.[4] While most affiliated with the national church, there were also Armenian Protestant denominations and a Roman Catholic church.

The church was by no means immune to the political conflicts in the Armenian community. In 1933 it experienced a violent schism. Archbishop Levon Tourian, appointed by the catholicos in Echmiadzin as the supreme prelate of the American Armenian church, already divided politically, stirred up a hornets' nest when he spoke at the Chicago World's Fair that summer. He appeared on a platform adorned with the tricolor of the defunct Armenian Republic. It was also, as it happened, the Dashnak banner. To both the catholicos and the Bolshevik government in Erevan it was considered an insult, and Archbishop Tourian refused to speak until the banner was removed. The Dashnaks flew into a rage. Nor were they appeased when the archbishop, thinking to apologize, said he had asked removal of the ensign out of respect for the regime in Armenia. This explanation further infuriated the Dashnaks, who sought to force Tourian's removal from his high office at the annual meeting of the National Church Council in September. The effort failed amidst debate on the legality of the proceeding. The meeting, nay the church, split into two factions. "The result was an Armenian Avignon," according to one bemused analyst.[5]

On December 24, 1933, at a church on West 187th Street in New York, the controversy reached a bloody climax vaguely reminiscent of the twelfth-century "murder in the cathedral" of Thomas à Becket, archbishop of Canterbury. As Archbishop Tourian, arrayed in the vestments of his office, proceeded to the altar to celebrate the divine liturgy, he was beset by two assassins and stabbed to death with a butcher knife. The American public, heretofore unaware of the brewing ecclesiastical conflict, was astonished by the front-page banner headline story in the *New York Times*.[6] Nine Dashnak partisans, known to have been in the church, were arrested for the crime. Two were tried and sentenced to death. In the absence of eyewitness testimony, the sentence was commuted to life in prison. The other seven received light prison sentences. The continuing division in the Armenian Church had little to do with religion. It was commonly described as a split between pro-Soviet and anti-Soviet factions in the Armenian community. The United States' recognition of the Soviet Union at the time of the schism undoubtedly dampened the ardor of the Dashnaks, but feelings thus aroused were not easily stilled. Ultimately, in 1956, the division would be recognized internationally by the designation of a second holy see, outside of Soviet Armenia, in Lebanon.

In 1934, not long before Christmas, Armenian Americans were thrilled by the publication in English translation of a historical novel, *The Forty Days of Musa Dagh,* they could read as a heroic epic of their genocidal ordeal and exile. The author, Franz Werfel, until now little known to American readers, was a Jewish Austrian born in Bohemia. During a sojourn at Damascus, as Werfel explained in a prefatory note, he had observed the plight of maimed and famished refugee children—Armenian orphans—in a carpet factory, and the sight gave him "the final impulse to snatch from the Hades of all that was, this incomprehensible destiny of the Armenian nation."[7] He found the historical story line of the novel in a factual report first published in the British blue book of 1916. However, for the Zeitun pastor, Dikran Andressian, Werfel substituted the fictional Gabriel Bagradian, a bourgeois cosmopolitan. He has made his home in Paris with a charming wife, Juliette, and their son, Stephan, who has no knowledge of his father's roots in Cilicia. Gabriel has returned to the family home in Yoghanolouk in 1914 on some business with his brother, who dies unexpectedly, while in the interim war descends on Turkey. Gabriel and his family are trapped. It becomes a defining moment for him, the moment when he rediscovers his Armenian identity. "Yesterday, for an instant," he reflects, "I felt unshakably convinced that I'd been brought here by some supernatural power, that God had something or other in store for me. My feeling really was unshakable, though it only lasted an instant. The life I've been living so far can't have been right." The story within the story of this stirring novel of valor and courage is the story of an exile's return and recovery of his national birthright.[8]

The book had the ring of authenticity for many Armenian Americans. With his fertile imagination Werfel introduces familiar details of the genocide into his narrative. One chapter, "Interlude of the Gods," draws on the Lepsius file to characterize the ruling triumvirs in Constantinople. Calling on Enver Pasha, the German missionary instantly saw the reason for the portraits of Frederick the Great and Napoleon on the wall. "Heroes five feet tall, little conquerors always on tip-toe, who force a way to power to spite their inches. Lepsius would have wagered anything that Enver Pasha wore high heels." When he offers eyewitness reports of Turkish atrocities, Enver asks his authority and Lepsius mentions Morgenthau. "'Mr. Morgenthau,' said Enver brightly, 'is a Jew. And Jews are always fanatically on the side of minorities.'"[9]

Most of the 817 pages of the novel are taken up with the Armenians' gallant defense of the mountain Musa Dagh against the Turkish assailants. It ends, of course, with the defenders' rescue by the French cruiser and other vessels. Werfel shortened the ordeal to forty days presumably because of the biblical associations of that number: Noah and the flood, Moses on Mount Sinai, the Israelites in the wilderness. The hero, Bagradian, chooses not to be rescued. He has lost his son, Stephan, in combat on Musa Dagh. The battle has become part of him. Wandering the cold and dark as the ships depart, he stops at Stephan's grave under a crude wooden cross. At that moment a soldier of the vengeful foe shoots him dead. "Gabriel Bagradian was lucky," the author writes: "The second Turkish bullet shattered his temple. He clung to the wood, tore it down with him. His son's cross lay on his heart."[10]

The Forty Days of Musa Dagh was an instant best-seller in the United States. Armenians hailed it for giving the nation a soul. In 1935 the book had been translated into twenty-four languages. It was purchased by Metro-Goldwyn-Mayer for $10,000 to be made into a major motion picture starring Clark Gable. The Turkish government protested vehemently, however; and with the timely intervention of the State Department, M-G-M agreed to cancel the movie, already in production, in return for fair financial compensation. This was a harbinger of the Ankara government's orchestrated campaign of denial of the genocide. Since that time no major Hollywood studio has been bold enough to produce *The Forty Days of Musa Dagh*.[11]

The novel acquired a certain immediacy because it appeared in the year Adolf Hitler came to power in Germany. It was banned and burned with all the other books by Jewish authors. At the margins of his consciousness, Werfel understood that his novel was inferentially about the plight of the Jews in Germany even though the story concerned the Armenians. Louis Kronenberg, reviewing the novel in the *New York Times Book Review,* did not fail to make the point. And in 1934, when the work appeared in Hebrew translation, it was quickly taken up and recognized by Jewish youth in Europe and Palestine as "a Jewish book"—not because the author was Jewish but because it addressed the condition and the fate of the Jews under the Nazi peril.[12]

For the next decade or so the Second World War and the events surrounding it overshadowed efforts of Armenian Americans to secure some kind of justice for the crimes of the Turkish genocide. In American opinion, generally, a cloud of silence fell over the subject. Soviet Armenians fought and died in the war together with their American cousins. At its close the USSR disavowed its friendship treaty with Turkey, a neutral in the conflict, then demanded cession of Kars and Ardahan, the strategic bastions taken from the Armenian Republic in 1920. Nationalists in the diaspora applauded this move as a forecast of the "greater" Armenia envisioned in President Wilson's abortive boundary proposal of that year. A new group, the American Committee for Justice to the Armenians, was formed to support repatriation to an Anatolian homeland. In those days Armenian meetings were apt to burst into the irredentist song "When Will We Get Back to Cilicia."[13] The USSR declined anything so adventurous, although it endorsed and encouraged Armenian repatriation from the diaspora to Soviet Armenia. Bright promises were held out to the repatriates, and several thousand Armenian Americans responded in the years after the war. Most of them, survivors of the genocide, were growing old and wished to live out their lives in the homeland. They were, for the most part, deeply disappointed with what they found. Writing in the *New York Times,* C. L. Sulzberger, in Geneva, estimated that 90 percent wanted to return to the United States, and many did. This was not the only Armenian repatriation during these years. Curiously, in 1947, 17,000 Armenians, refuse of the expulsion of Greeks and Armenians from Asia Minor a quarter-century earlier, were transported from Thessalonica to Batum.[14]

The United Nations had come into existence, and Armenian activists welcomed it as a new channel through which to advance their claims. Its predecessor, the League of Nations, had proved a disappointment. Armenian leaders badly needed an alternative channel to that of the State Department. They opposed the Truman Doctrine, announced by the president in March 1947, to extend U.S. economic and military aid to Greece and Turkey. (The Greeks were excepted from this opposition, however.) After the Hungarian uprising against Soviet domination in 1956, veterans of the American Committee for the Independence of Armenia, marking its thirty-ninth anniversary, did not fail to note the difference between the official American response to Hungarian nationalism and its earlier response to the Armenian variety.[15]

Although the word "genocide" has been used throughout this study, it did not come into existence until 1944, to describe the Nazi crime against the Jews. It was introduced in Article III of the indictment of the twenty-four Nazi leaders at Nuremberg in 1945. They were accused of "deliberate and systematic genocide," which accorded with the definition of Raphael Lemkin, the term's originator: the intentional extermination of a racial, religious, or ethnic group. The international genocide treaty followed in due course.

Henceforth, genocide came to mean a generic crime against humanity. And as the twentieth century progressed, it found wide global application from Cambodia to Rwanda. It well defined, as even Lemkin had recognized, the Turkish atrocity against the Armenians as well as the German atrocity against the Jews. The latter, however, proved of such unprecedented magnitude and uniqueness and so much writing and scholarship was gathered about it, in the opinion of historians, as to require its own name. And so "Holocaust," from the Greek meaning "whole burnt offering," entered the literature as a proper noun. The famous trial of Adolf Eichmann in Jerusalem in 1961 focused world opinion on the Jewish catastrophe. As it became known as the Holocaust, the little-remembered Turkish annihilation of the Armenians in the Great War took the name "genocide"—"the first genocide of the twentieth century"—and invited comparison with the Holocaust.[16]

Were authority wanted to associate and compare the Jewish Holocaust and the Armenian genocide, one had only to recall Adolf Hitler's appeal, nine days before the invasion of Poland, to the blood thirst of his commanding generals without fear of reprisal: "Who after all speaks today of the destruction of the Armenians?"[17] In both cases annihilation came about as the result of a deliberate political decision. Both were executed with bureaucratic cunning and system, though the Germans excelled in technology and their work was more efficient and complete. Both the Armenians and the Jews were ethnic minorities lacking statehood or sovereignty. Between the two sets of victims, however, there were important differences. While the alien character of both groups was the basic cause of their oppression, the anti-Semitism against the Jews was without parallel in Turkish feelings toward the Armenians. Religion, insofar as it was bound up with ethnic identity, was a critical factor in the Holocaust, while the sense of ethnic difference—the non-Turanism of the Armenians—seems to have been decisive in the genocide. The latter also represented an ideological conflict between opposing nationalisms. Both Jewish and Armenian survivors sought to save themselves and their respective cultures by total separation and independence from their oppressors.

Both, too, Jews and Armenians, sought remembrance, retribution, and requital as opportunities offered themselves over the years. Here the Jews were much more successful. They were well endowed and well organized. They already had their homeland. It became the sovereign state of Israel in 1948. They had Yad Vashem, dedicated to Jewish memory and survival. They had a classic victim of the Holocaust, Anne Frank, whose *Diary of a Young Girl* captured the world's heart upon its publication in 1947 and ever after. They had the great show trial of Adolf Eichmann in Jerusalem. As a Pole, Bohdan Gebarski, acutely observed to a Turkish friend: "All that Eichmann did to the Jews during 1942–1944 was the repetition on a larger scale of exactly what your countrymen inflicted on the Armenians in the year 1915 . . . the organized extermination of a people!"[18] But the Armenians had no Eichmann to dramatize the catastrophe to the world. Finally, and perhaps most important by way of comparison, the German nation offered repentance and reparation for its crimes, which the Turks have stonily refused to the Armenians.

By 1965, the fiftieth anniversary of the genocide, the parallel to the Holocaust was taking hold of the Armenian consciousness. April 24 became the worldwide day of remembrance observed by Armenians from that time forward. On that day in New York in 1965 Armenians repaired to their churches, marched from Washington Heights to the United Nations, and attended a memorial concert under the baton of Carl Karapetian at Lincoln Center. Similar observances took place in Los Angeles, Boston, and other cities with sizable Armenian communities, not alone in the United States but also in Paris, Beirut, and elsewhere. C. L. Sulzberger, the well-known foreign affairs correspondent of the *Times*, himself Jewish, declared the Armenians were "the Jews of World War I," and he called upon Turkey to acknowledge the genocide.[19]

In September 1966, *Commentary,* the formidable monthly of the American Jewish Committee, published an article, "The Unremembered Genocide," by Marjorie Housepian, a writer and teacher of English at Barnard College, who was also a student of Armenia's checkered past, which was truly a landmark in the revival of Armenian memory—perhaps of Jewish memory too—of the genocide. "Armenians," she wrote, "feel a tragic kinship with the Jewish people and have sought, often in vain, for a sign of acknowledgement of this bond." After reviewing the history of the tragedy, Housepian asked why the Turks were not held to account. "To put it in the simplest terms," she answered, "after Kemal Ataturk's victory in the Greco-Turkish War of 1920–22, every Western power, in its haste to beat its rivals to his favor . . . found one reason or another to absolve, or even exalt the Turkish nation." A veil descended on the bloody past. Even college textbooks portrayed Turkey as a noble twentieth-century success story.[20]

In 1957 the Armenian National Committee of America, a lobbying group, pressed the president of Turkey, then on a state visit to the United States, to place the oldest pending case of the crime of genocide on the agenda of the United Nations. Such a request only added to Turkish ill temper on the subject. Regardless, the Armenians eventually got their case before the U.N. Commission on Human Rights. Investigation of the matter was referred to the subcommittee on minorities. Upon presentation of an interim report in 1974, the Turkish representative on the commission objected to a crucial paragraph that read: "In modern times, attention should be drawn to the existence of fairly abundant documentation relating to the massacre of the Armenians, considered as 'the first genocide of the twentieth century.'" He labeled this statement propaganda and effectively torpedoed the Armenian initiative.[21]

Turkey's denial of the genocide was increasingly compared to the movement of Holocaust denial among Hitler's apologists and neo-Nazi parties. Denial, as Elie Wiesel observed, was like mur-

dering the victims a second time. More than that, it was the ultimate extinction of memory. To quote the historian Richard G. Hovannisian: "Denial is the final phase of genocide. Following the
physical destruction of a people and their national culture, memory is all that is left and [it] is targeted as the last victim. Complete
annihilation of a people requires the banishment of recollection
and the suffocation of remembrance."²² Turkish feelings were very
warm on anything touching Armenian memory of the genocide.
Nor were they limited to American offenses, such as the resolution
of the House of Representatives proclaiming a national day of remembrance of the catastrophe on its sixtieth anniversary. Two
years earlier, after learning of an allusion to the genocide engraved
on a monument in Marseilles, the Ankara government instantly recalled its ambassador to France. In Anatolia all physical remem-
brances of the Armenian people—monuments, schools, churches,
monasteries—were slated for destruction. It was said that churches
were targets for artillery practice by the Turkish army. Armenian
names gave way to Turkish. At the same time a major boulevard in
the capital, Ankara, was named for Talaat Pasha, and Istanbul, as
Constantinople was now called, boasted monuments to that
archcriminal. As Sulzberger observed, all this was in sharp contrast
to German behavior in the wake of the Holocaust, as indeed was
the substantial monetary reparations Germany made to Jewish survivors—an act never remotely emulated by the Turks.²³

Commemoration of the genocide, year after year, was a cata-
lyst to Armenian American recovery of a national past that was rapidly slipping away from them. In Watertown, Massachusetts, near
Boston, where one-fifth of the population was said to be Armenian, ambitious plans were laid in 1971 for the Armenia Library and
Museum of America. It became a standing witness against "suffocation of remembrance." In an earlier work of fiction about an Armenian American family, Marjorie Housepian noted the "cultural
extermination" experienced in America and remarked, "What our

enemies failed to do in fifteen hundred years our friends succeeded in doing in one generation." Survivor memoirs became a genre of Armenian literature; and scholars enriched the record with skillfully researched oral histories.[24] A pivotal book in 1972, by Dickran H. Boyajian, bore the title *Armenia: The Case for a Forgotten Genocide.* It combined documents with commentary in a somewhat disjointed history. The author hoped to awaken the dormant conscience of the civilized world to a monumental grievance and to lay out the case for an Armenian homeland.

Three years later appeared Michael Arlen's *Passage to Ararat.* Serialized in *The New Yorker* before publication as a book, it introduced or reintroduced a thoughtful American audience to the Armenian story. Yet in its way it was, like *The Forty Days of Musa Dagh,* about one man's rediscovery of his national identity, and so addressed the Armenian audience as well. Arlen, a writer well known as a film and television critic, was the son of an upscale cosmopolitan Armenian who had changed his name, forgotten his language, and utterly distanced himself from his heritage as he became a successful author. The son, at the age of forty, both parents gone, was by chance challenged to learn about the country that lay obscurely beyond Ararat. Still later he was persuaded by the famous author William Saroyan to journey to Armenia, as Saroyan himself had done, not once but often. And so at the age of sixty, as Arlen wrote, "I set out on a voyage to discover for myself what it is to be an Armenian." In Erevan everybody was Armenian. Arlen marveled over the antiquities in the great museum, the Matenadaran, and he was moved by the Monument to the Armenian Martyrs, with its eternal flame, high above the city. In the hands of a guide he traveled to other important cities and so got a broad-brush introduction to Soviet Armenia. Everywhere he went Arlen felt his father's presence. Unraveling the father's psyche, the son thought he had suffered the collective shame of a people that had been hunted unto death. Unable to confront it, he had buried disgrace deep in his subconscious mind. The voyage reconciled Michael Arlen psychologically with his father. It also opened a channel to his ethnic heritage, though Arlen realized that without having experienced the tragic ordeal of the nation he could never be an Armenian.[25]

The Armenian American community exhibited the generational pattern of assimilation common to the experience of immigrant groups. The first generation clings to the old ways, adapting slowly and hesitantly to the new culture in order to survive. The second generation, acclimated to that culture, shrugs off the old ways and rebels against the authority of tradition. The third generation typically seeks to recover what its parents forgot and to work out an accommodation with the immigrant heritage.[26]

Among the Armenians the revival of collective memory of the Turkish genocide was fulfilled in the third generation. Its members came of age about 1970. In 1975, as earlier noted, the House of Representatives, for the first time, passed a joint resolution calling for a National Day of Remembrance on April 24, the sixtieth anniversary of the genocide. The State Department objected lest it give offense to Turkey, a NATO (North Atlantic Treaty Organization) ally whose friendship was important to the security of the United States and the Western world. The resolution died in the Senate. Repeatedly over the years, as Turkish anger mounted, the same scenario was played out with minor variations. A national expression of sympathy for the Armenians—the once "starving Armenians"— was held hostage to NATO. Congressional hearings on these resolutions, dipping into the gruesome history, sometimes produced dismaying fireworks. In 1976, for example, Wayne Hays of Ohio revived the old canard that the Armenians were "sheep" for allowing themselves to be led to slaughter. Why should that be solemnly remembered by the American people? Scholars in attendance, such as UCLA's Richard Hovannisian and Boston University's Vahakn Dadrian, patiently tried to set the record straight.[27]

The year 1975 also marked the beginning of a wave of Armenian-led terrorism against Turkish diplomats in major European capitals—Vienna, Paris, Brussels, Lisbon—as well as Beirut and Istanbul. The aim, ostensibly, was to fix the world's attention on the unacknowledged and unredeemed crime of murder of one and a half million Armenians under Turkish authority in the First World War. Two underground groups, the Armenian Secret Liberation Army and the Justice Commandos of the Armenian Genocide, shared responsibility for the assassinations.[28] Parallels to contemporary terrorist groups in Italy, El Salvador, and Palestine were noted in the press. The United States was not immune to this virus of revenge. In fact, one of the earliest incidents, although free of conspiratorial motives, was the murder of the Turkish consul general and the vice consul in Santa Barbara, California, January 28, 1973. Gourgen N. Yanikian, a prominent seventy-seven-year-old land developer, still grief-stricken over the loss of twenty of his family in the genocide, freely confessed to the crime.[29]

The wave of international terrorism reached Los Angeles, home to almost 300,000 Armenians, on January 28, 1982. The Turkish consul, Kemal Ariken, was killed, and police arrested Harry Sassounian, nineteen years of age, on suspicion of murder. He was presently charged, tried, and convicted. The Justice Commandos took responsibility for the crime. California Attorney General George Deukmejian was in shock. Stanford J. Shaw, professor of Turkish Studies at UCLA, considered an apologist for the genocide by the Armenian Student Association, was placed under guard in the classroom. The editor of the *Los Angeles Times* proclaimed the political and moral "innocence" of the lamented consul, since his government had had no responsibility for the genocide. (Actually, international law assumes a successor government is liable for actions of its predecessors.) The editorial produced an avalanche of letters from readers maintaining that those who acquiesced in a crime against humanity shared the guilt of the perpetrators. The voices of 1.5 million dead could not be silenced forever. Later that year the FBI arrested four young Armenians of Los Angeles and a fifth from Boston on suspicion of terrorist acts.[30]

Not many Armenian Americans tried to justify terrorist acts, let alone advocated them, even those that had the character of targeted assassinations. The cry for revenge was a desperate plea for attention. In the absence of a tribunal to which the aggrieved might turn, unsurprisingly, some took revenge into their own hands. Some years later, in 1985, the Permanent Peoples' Tribunal, successor to Bertrand Russell's self-constituted tribunal on the Vietnam War, met in Paris to investigate and report on the Armenian genocide. Of course, it had no authority other than the conscience of its members, nor were there any accused to bring before the tribunal. So it had limited influence; but as long as Turkey remained in denial, such an expedient served as a last resort.[31]

On April 24, 1983, George Deukmejian, having been elected governor—the first Armenian American governor in the fifty states—spoke eloquently at the Los Angles Martyr Day ceremonies in Montebello, where some 7,000 people gathered at the Martyrs' Memorial. Armenians were united by bonds of pride and pain, he said. "We hurt together, we cry together and, yes, we are angry that year after year, decade after decade, the wrongs inflicted upon our people have gone unanswered and largely ignored." (Mayor Tom Bradley, the failed Democratic candidate in the gubernatorial race, made an appearance and quipped, "Next time, I will be campaigning as Tom Bradlibian.")[32]

In the ensuing years the issue again threaded its way into national politics. In 1985 President Ronald Reagan, himself a former California governor, seeking to assuage German feelings of guilt over the Holocaust, accepted an invitation to visit the German cemetery at Bitburg to honor the dead of World War II. Prominent among the graves were those of forty-nine Waffen SS officers who were the elite corps of the operation to annihilate the Jews. Elie

Wiesel, the celebrated author and survivor of Auschwitz, led an anguished protest against the president's gracing such a place. But to no avail. At the cemetery the president said that reconciliation was not forgetting, yet his presence seemed to convey a different message. Armenians could not dissociate this ceremonial act from the president's morally callous dissent to a National Day of Remembrance on the seventieth anniversary of the genocide in the same year. Again an appeal was made to the NATO alliance. But this time the president also offered the apology that consent to the memorial resolution could be construed as approval of the terrorist acts against Turkish diplomats. In other words, to condemn Turkish genocide in the past would be to endorse present-day revengeful acts. The logic of this statement eluded most observers, as the editor of the *Boston Globe* wrote. Behind the mask of antiterrorism, the president elevated expediency over morality.[33]

The following year Governor Deukmejian made a personal call on the State Department in behalf of the Remembrance Day resolution. He was unsuccessful, of course, yet found some satisfaction in the Senate's ratification, after thirty-seven years, of the U.N. Genocide Treaty. The *Los Angeles Times,* meanwhile, bowed to the outrage of the Armenian community by conceding the crucial point at issue between them.

> To put the Congress of the United States on record as deploring a human calamity still remembered with anguish is to strengthen the hand of the great majority in the Armenian community who seek redress through the legal process, not terror. To deny a cry for recognition that something dreadful happened in Armenia during a dreadful war was to embitter the agony of the memory.[34]

Armenian Americans distinguished themselves in every field of art and intellect. The first to make an indelible mark in the annals of

American literature was William Saroyan. Standing at the forefront of the second generation, he made his literary debut in *Hairenik* in 1933, at twenty-five years of age. His first book, *The Daring Young Man on the Flying Trapeze,* was published the following year. He had grown up in Fresno, in the San Joaquin Valley—the Armenian American heartland—the son of an immigrant father who had survived the massacre at Bitlis; now all the wit and humor, the anger and sadness of his people flowed from Saroyan's pen. In an early story, "Seventy Thousand Assyrians," he remembered from childhood the Near East Relief drives in Fresno. "My uncle used to be an orator and he used to make a whole auditorium full of Armenians weep." The reiterated laments "our own flesh and blood" and "homeless and starving" ended in the Job-like expostulation "Why is God angry at us!" In his first-person conversational style, Saroyan tells of getting a haircut from an Assyrian barber who doesn't want to be reminded of the civilization whence he came. After all, only 70,000 Assyrians are left on earth. We went in for all the wrong things, he says, like peace and quiet and family. "We didn't go in for machinery and conquest and militarism." Obviously, the story might have been a comment on the Armenians as well. Armenia was rarely Saroyan's expressed subject, yet one had the feeling he was always writing about it. Although he traveled to Soviet Armenia, Saroyan had little to say about it. His reticence may be explained by what he wrote in one of his stories, "The Armenian and the Armenian": "There is a small acre of land in Asia Minor that is called Armenia, but it is not so. It is not Armenia. It is a place. There are plains and mountains and rivers and lakes and cities in this place, and it is all fine . . . , but it is not Armenia." Armenia, presumably, was Fresno.[35]

As Margaret Bedrosian has observed, Saroyan was always puzzled by what it meant to be an Armenian as well as an American. The quandary was typical of the second generation. The Fresno schools, he wrote in retrospect, were in the business of turning out pattern Americans, and he rebelled. A teacher in one of his stories complains to him of the Armenians' clannish ways. They always stick together, she tells her pupil. He replies:

> "Don't you? All of you? Afraid of us? Our loud voices and swift ways? Don't you all stick together, too?"
> "Well, maybe we do, but then this *is* America, after all."
> "But we're here, too, now, and if you can't stand the only way we can be Americans, too, we'll go right on being Armenians."[36]

The rich tradition of Armenian poetry carried through the immigrant generations. David Kherdian, though some years younger than Saroyan, also falls into the second generation. His mother, of whom he wrote a memoir, was eight years old when she was deported from Harpoot; she lost her parents, everything, and finally reached America by way of Aleppo and Smyrna. Her son published a sheaf of elegiac poems, *Homage to Adana,* in 1970. One of the poems, "For My Father," captures the pathos and the inevitability of Americanization.

> Our trivial fights over spading
> the vegetable patch, painting
> the garden fence ocher instead of blue,
> and my resistance to Armenian food
> in preference for everything American,
> seemed, in my struggle for identity,
> to be the literal issue.
>
> Why have I waited until your death
> to know the earth you were turning
> was Armenia, the color of the fence
> your homage to Adana, and your
> other complaints over my own complaints

were addressed to your homesickness
brought on by my English.[37]

Many in the diaspora followed events in Soviet Armenia—the smallest republic of the USSR—with interest. Its population rose steadily, and it was among the freest and most prosperous of the Soviet republics, yet after the initial flurry of repatriation in the 1940s, very few Armenian Americans could be enticed to return there. The flow of immigration still ran the other way, facilitated by the lifting of national quotas in 1965. Nor has this situation changed since the collapse of the USSR. Hopes for the restored free and independent Armenian Republic in 1991 were dimmed by the devastating earthquake of 1989, followed by renewed warfare against the Tartars in mountainous Karabagh and Arctic-cold winters combined with an energy blockade by Azerbaijan. Besides, it was difficult for Armenian Americans to quarrel with their success in the United States. No immigrant group, it might be argued, achieved more upward mobility than the Armenians in the twentieth century.[38]

Robert Dole, majority leader of the Senate, with his wife, Elizabeth, soon to become head of the American Red Cross, visited the earthquake-stricken country in August 1989. The senator had a deep personal interest in Armenia. Dr. Hampar Kelikian, a Chicago surgeon of Armenian descent, had knitted together the broken bones his body suffered in combat in Italy during the Second World War; and out of gratitude to him Dole became a lifelong friend of the Armenian people. In 1990, not long after he returned home, the senator introduced the seventh in the series of resolutions praying for a national day of remembrance of the Armenian genocide. When it appeared likely the resolution would pass and that President George Bush might even sign it, Senator Robert Byrd, of West Virginia, vowed to filibuster the resolution to death. For three days the Senate was at a standstill. Finally, after the failure of two cloture votes, and responding to the pleas of colleagues, Dole withdrew the resolution.[39]

Years earlier the Turkish government had launched a counteroffensive against the claims of genocide. An Institute of Turkish Studies, in Washington, with the support of the Turkish ambassador, who had a basket of perquisites for congressmen, claimed the government had opened its archives to scholars, to have uncovered exculpatory documents, and to have won endorsement for its views from leading experts in Near Eastern history. Advertisements in the *New York Times* and the *Washington Post* in 1985, over the names of sixty-nine scholars, real or alleged, attested to the lie of the genocide.[40] Prominent among the signatories was Bernard Lewis, Cleveland E. Dodge Professor of Near Eastern History at Princeton University and author of *The Emergence of Modern Turkey,* a classic in the field, first published in 1961. Insofar as the work noticed the Turkish atrocities against the Armenians in the First World War, it was as "a struggle between two nations for the possession of a single homeland that ended with the terrible holocaust of 1916, when a million and a half Armenians perished."[41] Lewis later amplified this view in light of changing events. Because of Turkish partnership in NATO, he opposed agitation of the question of genocide lest it disrupt the alliance together with Turkish-American relations. This stance seemed to advance political expediency ahead of historical truth. In an interview in *Le Monde* in 1993, Lewis backed the admission of Turkey into the European Union, despite objections on account of genocide denial, among other reasons. Asked if *he* did not recognize the Armenian genocide, the professor responded, "You mean recognize the Armenian version of the story?" He then expounded the long-standing official view that Turkey acted in self-defense, and that newly uncovered documents proved an intent to banish, not to annihilate, the Armenians. Yves Ternon, the French scholar, with others, then declared that "Lewis had obviously left the field of scholarship and entered the arena of politics."

Ternon joined a civil suit brought in a French court claiming Lewis had forfeited his responsibility as a historian and shown disrespect for the Armenian people. A token verdict of guilty ran against Lewis. Meanwhile, a separate criminal suit, citing crimes against humanity under a law passed in the wake of the Nuremberg trials, was started but seems not to have been brought to conclusion.[42]

In the last decade of the twentieth century the question of genocide denial and responsibility became a matter of professional ethics in the American academy. Amy M. Rubin, in the *Chronicle of Higher Education,* disclosed a petition of scholars that charged the Turkish government of a campaign to corrupt the academy and manipulate history in order to enforce its view of the Armenian genocide. A year later a story in the *New York Times* accused Princeton of "fronting for the Turkish Government." The university had accepted a large gift from Ankara to establish an Atatürk Chair of Turkish Studies and had appointed as the first occupant Heath Lowry, who came from the position of executive director of the Washington-based Institute of Turkish Studies. Widely perceived as an apologist for Turkey, Lowry was known for, among other things, a celebrated gaff: the dismissal of Hitler's "Who today remembers the Armenians?" as "apocryphal," when it had, in fact, been confirmed by analysis of German cable traffic in 1939.[43]

From this noxious scandal one noted American university, the University of California at Los Angeles, emerged unscathed, or nearly so. The Turkish government had offered a gift of $1 million to found a chair in Turkish and Ottoman history. (It already had a chair in Armenian studies.) The university had taken a $250,000 down payment conditional on its final acceptance. Coming in the wake of the Princeton scandal, the proffered gift ignited controversy on the UCLA campus. One of the gift's conditions limited the search for an occupant of the chair to a scholar sympathetic to the Turkish view that the Armenians were the inadvertent casualties of war. Compliance with this condition, opponents charged, would make the university a dupe of Turkish propaganda. The History Department had the final voice on the question, and its faculty rejected the tendered gift by a vote of 18 to 17.[44] The debate, with the vote, was a climactic event in the Armenian American epoch. No amount of money could buy reconciliation without repentance.

Within the academy Armenian studies grew at a quickening pace toward the end of the century. The National Association for Armenian Studies and Research, founded in Belmont, Massachusetts, in 1955, saw to the endowment of professorships in more than a dozen American universities. From about 1970 a steady stream of scholarly monographs flowed from the presses; and archives have registered large collections of primary sources bearing on Armenian history. Two exemplary monuments of this endeavor may be singled out: Richard Hovannisian's four-volume *Republic of Armenia,* published over a period of twenty-five years by the University of California Press; and *Armenia: A Historical Atlas,* the work of Robert H. Hewsen under the sponsorship of the Armenian Center, Columbia University, and published in 2001 by the University of Chicago Press. Hewsen himself remarks in his introduction: "The growth and consolidation of the Armenian community in America in the past forty years has been paralleled by a growth in every aspect of the study of Armenia that has been nothing less than phenomenal."[45] And so, in this sense, the *Atlas,* which extends over four millennia, may by itself be considered a monument of American scholarship.

The year 1997 saw the publication of an arresting memoir, *Black Dog of Fate,* by the poet Peter Balakian. It, too, qualified as a memorial of an epoch. The author was born in 1951, the eldest of four children of a second-generation Armenian American family living in an affluent New Jersey suburb of New York City. His father was a respected and successful physician, his mother a college graduate; his adored aunts were teachers and writers; all of them were in love with America. The family suppressed memories of the cultural past. Between the parents Armenian was rarely spoken, and Peter, with the other children, was ignorant of the language. Only from his grandmother did he receive dim dreamlike echoes of Armenia. Should the name Armenia pop into conversation, it was quickly hushed up. Peter sometimes wished he were Jewish, as most of his school friends were, for they seemed to know exactly who they were. In the eighth grade he undertook a social studies project on Armenia at his father's suggestion. Going to the *World Book* and other sources at hand, he found virtually nothing, so he switched to a more promising subject, Turkey. He received an A on the paper, but his father was disappointed. "Don't you know what the Turks did to us?" he implored. "Would your Jewish friends write about the Germans like this?" Peter silently thought, Why hadn't he told me? Thereafter, as Peter went to prep school, then to college, Armenia occasionally reared up, but it formed, as the memoirist would write, only "a pattern of ruptured gestures between us."[46] What finally broke the logjam to Armenian memory was the chance discovery by an aunt of a "brittle manila envelope" containing the property claim and related papers his grandmother Nafina had prepared at Aleppo in 1920 on behalf of her husband, killed in 1915, and herself, a genocide survivor. This discovery, Peter Balakian said, "let me into the past." And he embarked on its rediscovery. By this time he was an aspiring poet and teacher. An early book of poems, *Sad Days of Light*, in 1983, led off with "The History of Armenia." It is a recollection of his grandmother, whose fragile memories had appeared to his child's mind like the flashing frames of a motion picture gone awry. The poet imagines the return of his grandmother in her brown dress along a highway under construction near East Orange, where they used to walk amid the steam hammers and bulldozers. Images from his grandmother's fragmented past fuse with the present. In a grocery store a butcher stands ankle-deep in blood; babies are eaten by the machines on the road; a garden is barren; fires rage through the suburbs.

> Grandpa is pressing
> pants, they came for him
> before the birds were up—
> he left without shoes
> or tie, without shirt
> or suspenders.
> It was quiet.
> The birds, the birds
> were still sleeping.

Balakian incorporated the poem in the pages of *Black Dog of Fate*.[47]

After some eighty years, the Armenian genocide remains a dark cloud over the human landscape, as Atom Egoyan's motion picture *Ararat,* in 2002, discloses in a stabbingly contemporary way. No doubt the rising generation of the Armenian American community will continue the quest for justice from the Turkish perpetrators of the genocide. That historic catastrophe will in the near future be showcased in the new Armenian Genocide Museum and Memorial, the project of the Armenian Assembly of America, just two blocks from the White House in Washington, D.C. Congress, meanwhile, will continue to be asked year after year to approve the Armenian Genocide Resolution and presidents will weigh it in the balance with realpolitik. A somewhat ludicrous piece of news came to children of the victims in 2001—a distant echo of Talaat's callous request to Henry Morgenthau in 1915. Eighty-five years after the event, the New York Life Insurance Company agreed to pay up to $10 million to heirs of its insured victims. The plaintiff, an eighty-five-year-old Californian, had been pressing the claim all his adult life.[48]

Coda

THE AWESTRUCK ANNALIST of the events recorded in these pages searches, finally, for a summation adequate to their meaning and significance in the human tragedy that is history. Tacitus, the great first-century Roman, declared that history's highest function is "to let no worthy action be uncommemorated, and to hold out the reprobation of posterity as a terror to evil words and deeds." By this standard, the historian cannot shirk the responsibility of moral judgment on the course of events that constitute his subject; and there can be no doubt where the judgment lies in this instance. But for that reprobation of the Turkish genocide upon the Armenians, Adolf Hitler may turn out to have been right after all about the world's easy forgetfulness.

The wholly unprecedented American humanitarian response to the Armenian genocide, though soon forgotten, merits a permanent place in American memory. It lit a candle before "the blackest page in history" and sustained the surviving remnant of the Armenian people amid tumultuous waste and destruction. The Christian leitmotiv of the effort was a late expression of an impulse ingrained in the American tradition. The movement failed to achieve its secular objective: a viable free and independent republic of Armenia in the Near East, under the fostering care of the United States. "What hopes were centered on Armenia!" one of the missionaries exclaimed. "The hopeless heartbreak is so much the more poignant."

Armenia must be reckoned a diplomatic failure of the United States, indeed of the European Allies as well. Yet because of the lifeline of Near East Relief and the ebb and flow of immigration, an Armenian American community took root and flourished in this country from Boston to Fresno and beyond. That community is at once a tribute to the talents and the staying power of a remarkable people and to the freedom, the openness, and the opportunities of this new found land.

Notes

Abbreviations

ABC Papers   Papers of the American Board of Commissioners for Foreign Missions, Houghton Library, Harvard University

NYT   *New York Times*

Prologue

1. Henry Morgenthau, *All in a Life-Time* (Garden City, N.Y., 1922), 160.
2. Oscar Straus, *Under Four Administrations from Cleveland to Taft* (Boston, 1922), 297.
3. Morgenthau, *All in a Life-Time*, 176.
4. Henry Morgenthau, *Ambassador Morgenthau's Story* (Garden City, N.Y., 1918), chap. 2; Lewis Einstein, *Inside Constantinople: A Diplomatist's Diary during the Dardanelles Expedition* (London, 1917), 1.
5. Morgenthau, *All in a Life-Time*, 209, 203.
6. Einstein, *Inside Constantinople*, 2.
7. See Ulrich Trumpener, *Germany and the Ottoman Empire, 1914–1918* (Princeton, 1968), 13 and passim.
8. Morgenthau, *Ambassador Morgenthau's Story*, 161–70, 195; Einstein, *Inside Constantinople*, vii.
9. Clarence D. Ussher, *An American Physician in Turkey* (Boston, 1917), 280; Morgenthau, *Ambassador Morgenthau's Story*, 299.
10. Morgenthau, *Ambassador Morgenthau's Story*, 313–14.
11. Leslie Davis to Henry Morgenthau, June 30, 1915, quoted in Armen Hairopetian, "Race Problems and the Armenian Genocide: The State Department File," *Armenian Review* 37 (Spring 1984): 48.
12. Morgenthau, *Ambassador Morgenthau's Story*, 290, 333–34, 337, 339.
13. Einstein, *Inside Constantinople*, 176; Morgenthau, *Ambassador Morgenthau's Story*, 383, 343; Trumpener, *Germany and the Ottoman Empire*, 220–42.

14. Morgenthau to Secretary of State, Apr. 27, July 20, and Aug. 11, 1915, in *Foreign Relations of the United States,* 1915 supp. (Washington, D.C., 1928), 980, 982–83, 986, 988.

15. Ibid., 988.

16. James L. Barton, *The Story of Near East Relief* (New York, 1930), 4–9.

17. *NYT,* Oct. 4, 1915.

18. Barton, *Story of Near East Relief,* 385, 391–92, 328.

1. Awakening

1. Akaby Nassibian, *Britain and the Armenian Question, 1915–1923* (New York, 1984), 34–35; William Yale, *The Near East: A Modern History* (Ann Arbor, 1958), 85–87; Christopher J. Walker, *Armenia: The Survival of a Nation,* 2d ed. (London, 1990), 106–17.

2. Walker, *Armenia,* 116.

3. Sarkis Atamian, *The Armenian Community* (New York, 1955), 43–44.

4. Sir Charles Eliot, *Turkey in Europe* (New York, 1965), 407.

5. Ibid., 390–91.

6. H. F. B. Lynch, *Armenia: Travels and Studies* (Beirut, 1965), 1:456.

7. Quoted in Hagop Martin Deranian, "'Worcester Is America,'" *Journal of Armenian Studies* 3 (1986–87): 15; John De Nova, *American Interests and Politics in the Middle East, 1900–1939* (Minneapolis, 1963), 114. See also Joseph L. Grabill, *Protestant Diplomacy and the Near East: Missionary Influence on American Policy, 1810–1927* (Minneapolis, 1971).

8. Edwin M. Bliss, *Turkey and the Armenian Atrocities* (Fresno, 1982), 303. See also William Nesbitt Chambers, *Yoljuk: Random Thoughts on a Life in Imperial Turkey* (London, 1928), 101–2.

9. John Minassian, *Many Hills Yet to Climb* (Santa Barbara, 1986), 8.

10. Sir Edwin Pears, *Forty Years in Constantinople* (London, 1916), 151.

11. For Riggs, see Grabill, *Protestant Diplomacy,* 21 and passim; Grace H. Knapp, *The Tragedy of Bitlis* (New York, 1919); Barbara J. Merguerian, "Mt. Holyoke Seminary in Bitlis," *Armenian Review* 43 (Spring 1990): 31–65; Caleb Frank Gates, *Not to Me Only* (Princeton, 1940).

12. Yale, *Near East,* 122–23; Walker, *Armenia,* 68–69.

13. Pears, *Forty Years in Constantinople,* 103.

14. Vahakn N. Dadrian, *The History of the Armenian Genocide: Ethnic Conflict from the Balkans to Anatolia to the Caucasus* (Providence, 1995), 117; Walker, *Armenia,* 136–42.

15. Walker, *Armenia,* 153; Pears, *Forty Years in Constantinople,* 103, 161.

16. Ephraim K. Jernagian, *Judgment unto Truth: Witnessing the Armenian Genocide,* trans. Alice Haig (New Brunswick, 1990), 37.

17. Walker, *Armenia,* 167, 164–70.

18. Dadrian, *History of the Armenian Genocide,* 124, 155.

19. *NYT,* Nov. 17, 1894.

20. Clara Barton, *The Red Cross in Peace and War* (Washington, D.C., 1898), 275–349.

21. See, in general, Atamian, *Armenian Community,* 353–54; M. Vartan Malcolm, *The Armenians in America* (Boston, 1919), 62; Robert Mirak, *Torn between Two Lands: Armenians in America, 1890 to World War I* (Cambridge, 1983).

22. *Outlook* 124 (1920): 319–20; James W. Gerard, Introduction to Malcolm, *Armenians in America;* Mirak, *Torn between Two Lands,* passim.

23. Osip Mandelstam, *Journey to Armenia,* trans. Sidney Manas (San Francisco, 1979), 42.

2. Genocide

1. Quoted in Rubina Peroomian, *Literary Responses to Catastrophe* (Atlanta, 1993), 91. See especially W. Nesbitt Chambers, "Account of Adana Massacre," 1969, in ABC Papers, n.s. 6.13.25.

2. Robert Melson, *Revolution and Genocide: On the Origins of the Armenian Genocide and the Holocaust* (Chicago, 1992), 138. See also Yves Ternon, *The Armenians: History of a Genocide,* trans. Rouben C. Chalokian (Delmar, N.Y., 1981), 163–68.

3. Quoted in Christopher J. Walker, *Armenia: The Survival of a Nation* (London, 1990), 207, 200–201.

4. Ibid., 203–4, 209. On Van see especially Rafael de Nogales, *Four Years beneath the Crescent,* trans. Muna Lee (New York, 1926), chap. 6.

5. The text is included in *The Treatment of the Armenians in the Ottoman Empire, 1915–16,* ed. James Bryce (London, 1916), 659–60.

6. Dickran H. Boyajian, *Armenia: The Case for a Forgotten Genocide* (New York, 1972), 104–5. The author draws upon Johannes Lepsius, *Deutschland und Armenia, 1914–1918.*

7. Bryce, *Treatment of the Armenians,* 222–23, 229, 231.

8. Ibid., 285, 286–87.

9. Ibid., 290–92.

10. H. F. B. Lynch, *Armenia: Travels and Studies* (Beirut, 1965), 391.

11. Leslie A. Davis, *The Slaughterhouse Province,* ed. Susan Blair (New Rochelle, N.Y., 1989), 52.

12. Henry H. Riggs, *Days of Tragedy in Armenia* (Ann Arbor, 1997), 124. See also Riggs's typescript, "History of the Mission to Turkey, 1910–1942," ABC 88.

13. Riggs, *Days of Tragedy,* 90–93; Davis, *Slaughterhouse Province,* 54–57.

14. Quoted in *United States Official Documents on the Armenian Genocide,* comp. Ara Sarafian, 3 vols. (Watertown, Mass., 1993–95), 1:53.

15. Davis, *Slaughterhouse Province,* 59; Riggs, *Days of Tragedy,* 93.

16. Bryce, *Treatment of the Armenians,* 265–67.

17. Riggs, *Days of Tragedy,* 96, 131.

18. Bryce, *Treatment of the Armenians,* 265–67.

19. *U.S. Official Documents,* 1:130.

20. Davis, *Slaughterhouse Province,* 84–87.

21. Riggs, *Days of Tragedy,* 131. And see Maria Jacobsen, *Diaries of a Danish Missionary: Harpoot, 1907–1919,* trans. Kristen Vind (Princeton, 2001).

22. Davis to Morgenthau, Dec. 30, 1915, in *Slaughterhouse Province,* 183.
23. Ternon, *Armenians,* 150, 258; Abraham Hartunian, *Neither to Laugh nor to Weep: A Memoir of the Armenian Genocide,* trans. Vartan Hartunian (Boston, 1968), 91; John Minassian, *Many Hills Yet to Climb: Memoirs of an Armenian Deportee* (Santa Barbara, 1986), 193.
24. Bryce, *Treatment of the Armenians,* 466, 512–20.
25. Ibid., 518–19, 629, 519–20; J. B. Jackson to Secretary of State, May 27, 1918, in *U.S. Official Documents,* 1:159.
26. Bryce, *Treatment of the Armenians,* 532; Ephraim K. Jernagian, *Judgment unto Truth: Witnessing the Armenian Genocide,* trans. Alice Haig (New Brunswick, 1990), 87–88.
27. *NYT,* Oct. 22, 1916.
28. William H. Rockwell, in *Current History,* Nov. 16, 1916, 337–38.
29. Martin Niepage, *The Horrors of Aleppo* (London, 1916), 7. See also Mikran T. Kaloidjian, in *NYT,* April 4, 1918; and Lillian Elanekjian, "Toynbee, Turks, and Armenians," *Armenian Review* 37 (Summer 1984): 62–65.
30. Naim Bey, *The Memoirs of Naim Bey,* comp. Aram Andonian (London, [1920]), ix, 7, 58, 60, 66, 69, and passim. See also Vahakn N. Dadrian, "The Naim-Andonian Documents on the World War I Destruction of Ottoman Armenians: The Anatomy of a Genocide," *International Journal of Middle East Studies* 18 (1986): 311–60. This study maintains the validity of the Naim evidence in the face of arguments of Turkish scholars to the contrary.
31. Vahakn N. Dadrian, *The History of the Armenian Genocide: Ethnic Conflict from the Balkans to Anatolia to the Caucasus* (Providence, 1995), 124.
32. Quoted in Herbert Adams Gibbons, *The Blackest Page of Modern History* (New York, 1916), 30; Bryce, *Treatment of the Armenians,* 258.
33. Bryce, *Treatment of the Armenians,* 258.
34. Quoted in James L. Barton, *Story of Near East Relief* (New York, 1930), 222n.
35. Melson, *Revolution and Genocide,* 138.
36. Bryce, *Treatment of the Armenians,* 504.

3. Near East Relief in War and Peace

1. Joseph L. Grabill, "Cleveland H. Dodge, Woodrow Wilson, and the Near East," *Journal of Presbyterian History* 48 (1970): 249–64; and Grabill, *Protestant Diplomacy and the Near East: Missionary Influence on American Policy, 1910–1927* (Minneapolis, 1971). James L. Barton's reminiscences appeared in *Missionary Herald* 123 (1927).
2. See Robert Mirak, *Torn between Two Lands: Armenians in America* (Cambridge, 1983).
3. Woodrow Wilson to Henry Morgenthau, May 23, 1916, in Morgenthau Papers: General Correspondence, Library of Congress.
4. James L. Barton, *The Story of Near East Relief* (New York, 1930), 55.
5. Ibid., 14.
6. Ibid., 65.

7. *NYT,* Oct. 15, 1916; May 28 and July 18, 1917; Barton, *Story of Near East Relief,* 64.

8. Lorin Shephard to Enoch Bell, Aug. 24, 1919, in ABC Papers, Central Turkey Mission, Microfilm Edition, Reel 672, Houghton Library, Harvard University.

9. Frederick W. MacCallum to James L. Barton, Nov. 26, 1917, and Nishan Hagopian, "The Work among the Refugees Done by the Armenian Relief Committee," both in ABC Papers, Western Turkey Mission, Reel 632.

10. Anna Harlow Birge to James L. Barton, Nov. 22, 1915, and George E. White to Enoch Bell, Aug. 20, 1917, ibid., Reels 630 and 636.

11. Edith Cold to Mrs. Lee, June 12, 1915, in ABC Papers, Central Turkey Mission, Reel 670.

12. *News Bulletin of the American Committee for Armenian and Syrian Relief,* June 1918.

13. John H. Finley Papers, in Near East Relief Correspondence, Box 31, New York Public Library.

14. *News Bulletin,* September 1918.

15. *NYT,* Aug. 10 and 19, Oct. 29, and Dec. 12, 1917; *News Bulletin,* September 1918.

16. *News Bulletin,* September 1918.

17. Anthony Slide, comp., *Ravished Armenia and the Story of Aurora Mardiganian* (Lanham, Md., 1997).

18. Ibid.; *Ravished Armenia: The Story of Aurora Mardiganian* (New York, 1918).

19. *NYT,* April 8, 1918.

20. Ibid., June 22, 1918.

21. Richard G. Hovannisian, *Armenia and the Road to Independence, 1918* (Berkeley, 1967), 201.

22. *NYT,* Nov. 6, 1918 (Morgenthau); Oct. 11, Nov. 25, and Dec. 7 and 8, 1918.

23. Robert Lansing to Joseph Tumulty, Nov. 22, 1918, and Wilson to Pope Benedict XV, Dec. 24, 1918, in *The Papers of Woodrow Wilson,* ed. Arthur Link et al., 69 vols. (Princeton, 1966–94), 53:420n, 489.

24. Barton, *Story of Near East Relief,* 107–11.

25. Frederick W. MacCallum to Barton, Nov. 23, 1918, in ABC Papers, Western Turkey Mission, Reel 632; John H. Kingsbury to ACRNE, March 1919, ibid.; George E. White to Enoch Bell, Apr. 19, 1919, and White to Barton, June 22, 1919, ibid., Reel 636. For Maria Jacobsen see the leaflet of the Massachusetts Committee for Near East Relief, *Harpoot: The City of Homeless Children,* no. 258, in ABC Papers; and also Jacobsen's *Diary of a Danish Missionary* (Princeton, 2001), 207 and passim.

26. Esther Greene to Mrs. Emerson, Dec. 2, 1919, in Papers of the Smith College Relief Unit, Sophia Smith Collection, Box 160, Smith College.

27. Laurence Evans, *United States Policy and the Partition of Turkey, 1914–1924* (Baltimore, 1965), 71–81.

28. Robert Lansing, *The Peace Negotiations: A Personal Narrative* (Boston, 1921), 59, 160.

29. Houri Beberian, "The Delegation of Integral Armenia," *Armenian Review* 44 (1991): 39–64.

30. Quoted in Stephen Bonsal, *Suitors and Supplicants: The Little Nations at Versailles*

(New York, 1946), 186; Walter Duranty in *NYT,* Jan. 19, 1919; Morgenthau, Diary, Aug. 22, 1917, in Morgenthau Papers, Library of Congress.

31. *Congressional Record,* 65th Cong., 2d sess., Appendix, 168.
32. James Bryce, "The Future of Armenia," *Contemporary Review* 114 (1918): 604–11; and see H. A. L. Fisher, *James Bryce* (New York, 1927), 2:211–12 and passim.
33. *New Republic,* Sept. 10, 1919, 163–64; *NYT,* Feb. 16, 1919.
34. Lewis Einstein, "The Armenian Mandate," *Nation,* June 5, 1920, 762–63.
35. Secret Memo, Imperial War Cabinet, Dec. 30, 1918, in *Papers of Woodrow Wilson,* 53:561–62.
36. *Chicago Tribune,* Feb. 24, 1919.
37. Joseph Tumulty, *Woodrow Wilson as I Knew Him* (New York, 1921), 375–77.
38. Melville Chater, "The Land of Stalking Death," *National Geographic,* January, 1919, 393–420.
39. Herbert Hoover, *An American Epic,* 3 vols. (Chicago, 1959–61), 3:201, 203–7; John Elder, "Memoir of the Armenian Republic," *Armenian Review* 6 (March 1953): 3–27.
40. Hoover to Morgenthau, June 14, 1919, in Morgenthau Papers: General Correspondence, Library of Congress.
41. Richard G. Hovannisian, *The Republic of Armenia,* 4 vols. (Berkeley, 1972–96), 2:40–48; Thomas A. Bryson, *Walter George Smith* (Washington, D.C., 1977), 101–8. For the repatriation plan, see "Statement to President of the Council of Ministers," Peace Conference, Paris, July 2, 1919, in ABC Papers: Clarence D. Ussher Papers and Correspondence.
42. Ernest A. Yarrow to a friend, July 30, 1919, in Yarrow Papers, ABC 76, Box 1.
43. A. Rawlinson, *Adventures in the Near East* (New York, 1924), 143, 252, 186, 189.
44. *NYT,* Sept. 24, 1919.
45. Ibid., Aug. 26 and 19, 1919.
46. Quoted in Hovannisian, *Republic of Armenia,* 2:114.
47. James H. Tashjian, ed., "Life and Papers of Vahan Cardashian," *Armenian Review* 11 (Spring 1958): 62–63; John R. Mardick, "Life and Times of Vahan Cardashian," ibid. 10 (Spring 1957): 3–15.
48. For ACIA see Gregory L. Aftandilian, *Armenia, Vision of a Republic: The Independence Lobby in America, 1918–1927* (Boston, 1981). Neither of Gerard's biographical works treats his leadership of ACIA.
49. For Cardashian on the issue, see *NYT,* May 1, May 23, June 3, and June 5, 1919; Bliss is quoted in Hovannisian, *Republic of Armenia,* 2:322.
50. *NYT,* May 25, 1919.
51. Ibid., July 6, 1919.
52. Cardashian letter, *NYT,* May 1, 1919; Aftandilian, *Armenia,* 31–35.
53. Frank E. Manuel, *The Realities of American-Palestine Relations* (Washington, D.C., 1949), 134. See also Howard M. Sachar, *The Emergence of the Middle East, 1914–1924* (New York, 1969), which is perceptive on Armenia.

54. Harry N. Howard, *The King-Crane Commission* (Beirut, 1963), 160, 182–94. See also James B. Gidney, *A Mandate for Armenia* (Oberlin, 1967), chap. 7.

55. Hovannisian, *Republic of Armenia*, 2:330–33; *NYT*, Dec. 3 and 4, 1922.

56. *Papers of Woodrow Wilson*, 63:71, 304, 458.

57. U.S. Senate, Subcommittee on Foreign Relations, *Hearings: Maintenance of Peace in Armenia*, 66th Cong., 1st sess. (Washington, D.C., 1919).

58. Ibid.; Hovannisian, *Republic of Armenia*, 2:389–90.

59. Ibid., 387; *Boston Globe*, Dec. 14, 1919.

60. *NYT*, Dec. 8, 1919.

4. Chaos, Carnage, and Survivors

1. *Congressional Record*, 66 Cong., 2d sess., 3907.

2. Stanley E. Kerr, *The Lions of Marash: Personal Experiences with American Near East Relief, 1919–1922* (Albany, 1973), Preface; Richard G. Hovannisian, *The Republic of Armenia*, 4 vols. (Berkeley, 1972–96), 2:416.

3. *NYT*, Apr. 19, 1919.

4. Winston S. Churchill, *The World Crisis: The Aftermath* (London, 1929), 368.

5. Halidé Ebib, *The Turkish Ordeal* (New York, 1928), 185.

6. Kerr, *Lions of Marash*, 97.

7. Mabel Evelyn Elliott, *Beginning Again at Ararat* (New York, 1924), 99, 101, 103, and chap. 7.

8. Ibid., chap. 8; see also *NYT*, June 21, 1920.

9. Christopher J. Walker, *Armenia: The Survival of a Nation*, rev. ed. (London, 1990), 297, 303; Alice Keep Clark, *Letters from Cilicia* (Chicago, 1924); Mrs. D. C. Eby, *At the Mercy of Turkish Brigands* (New Carlisle, Ohio, 1922); *NYT*, Nov. 2, 1920; Merrill is quoted in "Agony of a City: The 314 Days of Aintab," *Armenian Review* 30 (Summer 1977): 122.

10. *NYT*, June 16 and Oct. 9, 1920.

11. James L. Barton to W. W. Peet, Mar. 5, 1920, Missionary Book 315, in ABC Papers; Mark L. Bristol Diary, in Mark L. Bristol Papers, Library of Congress, July 20 and Nov. 9, 1919; June 7 and Sept. 2, 1920; Oct. 24, 1926; and Lawrence W. Evans, *United States Policy and the Partition of Turkey, 1914–1924* (Baltimore, 1965), 182–83.

12. Walker, *Armenia*, 302.

13. Lord Kinross, *Ataturk: A Biography of Mustafa Kemal, Father of Modern Turkey* (New York, 1965), 325–26.

14. Robert Underwood Johnson, *Remembered Yesterdays* (Boston, 1923), 528–30.

15. James W. Gerard to Wilson, May 14, 1920, in *The Papers of Woodrow Wilson*, ed. Arthur S. Link et al., 69 vols. (Princeton, 1966–94), 65:288.

16. See Hovannisian, *Republic of Armenia*, 2:356–64. The Harbord Report appears in the *Congressional Record* as Senate Document 264, 66th Cong., 2d sess.

17. *NYT*, Apr. 11, 1920 (Hoover), and Apr. 6, 1920 (editorial).

18. Quoted in Wesley N. Bagby, *The Road to Normalcy: The Presidential Campaign of 1920* (Baltimore, 1962), 23.
19. Clarence Day Jr., "The Everlasting Armenians," *Harper's Magazine,* January 1920, 281–84.
20. *NYT,* May 3, 1920.
21. Woodrow Wilson to Cleveland H. Dodge, Apr. 19, 1920, in *Papers of Woodrow Wilson,* 65:202.
22. Wilson to Bainbridge Colby, May 11, 1920, and Colby to Wilson, May 20, 1920, ibid., 271–72, 306.
23. Quoted in Hovannisian, *Republic of Armenia,* 4:13.
24. Message to Congress, May 24, 1920, in *Papers of Woodrow Wilson,* 65:520–23.
25. On the debate, see Hovannisian, *Republic of Armenia,* 4:15–24. See also James B. Gidney, *A Mandate for Armenia* (Oberlin, 1967), chap. 10 and passim.
26. *NYT,* June 11, 1920; Lodge quoted in Allen Nevins, *Henry White: Thirty Years of American Diplomacy* (New York, 1930), 466.
27. *NYT,* May 26, 1920.
28. Thomas A. Bryson, "Woodrow Wilson and the Armenian Mandate: A Reassessment," *Armenian Review* 21 (Fall 1968): 10–29.
29. From the diary of Ray Stannard Baker, Nov. 28, 1920, in *Papers of Woodrow Wilson,* 56:435.
30. "A Memorandum by Carter Glass," ibid., 65:435–36n.
31. Hovannisian, *Republic of Armenia,* 4:44n; Bristol Diary, Dec. 19, 1920. The document "The Frontier between Armenia and Turkey as Described by President Wilson" appears in *Armenian Review* 19 (Summer 1966): 3–16; *NYT,* Jan. 3, 1921.
32. Quoted in Rita Jerrabian, "Abandonment of the Armenian Question as an International Issue," *Armenian Review* 9 (Winter 1956): 115.
33. Quoted in Walker, *Armenia,* 320n; in general, 306–22. See also Oliver Baldwin, *Six Prisons and Two Revolutions* (New York, 1925), chaps. 2 and 8; and the discussion in Hovannisian, *Republic of Armenia,* 4:390–402; also Manoug Joseph Somakian, *Empires in Conflict: Armenia and the Great Powers, 1895–1920* (London, 1995), 236–42.
34. *NYT,* Dec. 24, 1920; also Nov. 24 and 26, 1920; and Viscount [Robert] Cecil, *A Great Experiment: An Autobiography* (New York, 1941), 113, 35.
35. See Joseph L. Grabill, *Protestant Diplomacy in the Near East: Missionary Influence on American Policy, 1910–1927* (Minneapolis, 1971), 249–63; and Thomas A. Bryson, *Walter George Smith* (Washington, 1977), 128–35, 144.
36. *New Near East,* July–August, 1920.
37. Ibid., February 1921.
38. Ibid., October 1920 (Vickrey), September 1920 (Knox).
39. Ernest A. Yarrow to Commissar of Alexandropol, in *Papers Relating to the Foreign Relations of the United States, 1919* (Washington, D.C., 1934), 2:928–29; James L. Barton, *Story of Near East Relief* (New York, 1930), 128–31; *New Near East,* December 1920.
40. Quoted in Barton, *Story of Near East Relief,* 129–30.

41. Ibid., 131.
42. Ibid., 132–36; *Papers Relating to Foreign Relations,* 2:931; Barton to Yarrow, May 6, 1921, in Yarrow Papers, ABC 76, Box 2.
43. Elliott, *Beginning Again at Ararat,* 174.
44. Esther Pohl Lovejoy, *Certain Samaritans,* rev. ed. (New York, 1933), 119, 121, 123.
45. *New Near East,* July 1921, September 1922.
46. Lovejoy, *Certain Samaritans,* 126–27; *New Near East,* February and April 1922.
47. *New Near East,* November 1921, November 1922, June 1922.
48. Ibid., January 1923, November 1922.
49. Ibid., February 1922.
50. Ibid., November 1921.
51. Ibid., February 1921.
52. Ibid., June 1921.
53. Bristol Diary, June 25, 1921.
54. *New Near East,* December 1921.
55. Ibid., Jan. 1922; Elliott, *Beginning Again at Ararat,* 341.

5. The Great Betrayal

1. The principal accounts are Jacques Derogy, *Resistance and Revenge: The Armenian Assassination of the Turkish Leaders Responsible for the 1915 Massacres and Deportations,* trans. A. M. Berrett (New Brunswick, 1990); and Edward Alexander, *A Crime of Vengeance: An Armenian Struggle for Justice* (New York, 1991). Yet another work, on the secret Dashnak campaign to eliminate the Ittihad leaders, is Arshavir Sheragian, *The Legacy: Memoirs of an Armenian Patriot,* trans. Sonia Sheragian (Boston, 1976).
2. Alexander, *Crime of Vengeance,* 70, 76, 186, passim; Derogy, *Resistance and Revenge,* chap. 6; *Armin T. Wegner and the Armenians in Anatolia, 1915* (Milan, 1996), 147–54, 16.
3. Alexander, *Crime of Vengeance,* 203.
4. Kemal is quoted in *Armenian Review* 25 (Autumn 1972): 78. On Enver, see David Fromkin, *A Peace to End All Peace* (New York, 1989), 429–30, 480.
5. Vahakn N. Dadrian, *The History of the Armenian Genocide: Ethnic Conflict from the Balkans to Anatolia to the Caucasus* (Providence, 1995), 318. See also James F. Willis, *Prologue to Nuremberg* (Westport, Conn., 1982).
6. *NYT,* Apr. 14 and 20, 1919.
7. *New Near East,* March and May 1922.
8. *Literary Digest,* April 15, 1922, 17; *NYT,* Apr. 13 and 14, 1922.
9. Quoted in Derogy, *Resistance and Revenge,* 95.
10. On the Pontine Greeks, see particularly Thea Halo, *Not Even My Name* (New York, 2000), bk. 3.
11. [Charles T. Riggs], "History of Merzifon Station," in ABC Papers 88; George E. White to James L. Barton, Oct. 30, 1922; White to William W. Peet, Nov. 7, 1922;

and White to Ernest Riggs, Jan. 24, 1923, all ibid., Western Turkey Mission, Letters, 1920–24, vol. 3.

12. Barton to Peet, Dec. 30, 1921; Feb. 3, Mar. 3, and Mar. 7, 1922, all ibid., Western Turkey Mission, Letterbooks; Peet to Barton, Dec. 8, 1921; Feb. 2 and 9, 1922, all ibid., Letters; Mark L. Bristol Diary, Oct. 21, 1919, in Mark L. Bristol Papers, Library of Congress.

13. Forest D. Yowell to Consul Jackson, Apr. 5, 1922, in U.S. State Department Papers, no. 528, Microfilm 353, Roll 47, National Archives. See also Bristol Diary, May 3, 1922.

14. *Christian Science Monitor*, May 19, 23, 24, 29, and 31, June 2 and 5, 1922; *NYT*, May 6 and June 4, 1922. See also Levon Marashlian, "Finishing the Genocide," in *Remembrance and Denial: The Case of the Armenian Genocide*, ed. Richard G. Hovannisian, chap. 4 (Detroit, 1998); Admiral Mark L. Bristol to U.S. State Department, May 22, 1922, Microfilm Roll 2, and Mary Caroline Holmes to Admiral Bristol, May 29, 1922, Microfilm Roll 48, both in U.S. State Department Papers, National Archives. See also Florence Billings Papers in Sophia Smith Collection, Smith College.

15. *Papers Relating to the Foreign Relations of the United States*, 1922 (Washington, D.C., 1934), 2:922; *NYT*, May 25, 1922.

16. See especially Marjorie Housepian, *Smyrna, 1922: The Destruction of a City* (London, 1972).

17. Abraham H. Hartunian, *Neither to Laugh nor to Weep: A Memoir of the Armenian Genocide*, trans. Vartan Hartunian (Boston, 1968), 199.

18. Quoted in Housepian, *Smyrna*, 166–67.

19. Ibid., 201n; George Horton, *The Blight of Asia* (Indianapolis, 1926), 112.

20. Esther Pohl Lovejoy, *Certain Samaritans*, rev. ed. (New York, 1933), 147–48; Housepian, *Smyrna*, 189–97.

21. The aide-mémoire is conveniently summarized in Joseph C. Grew, *Turbulent Era: A Diplomat's Record of Forty Years, 1904–1945*, ed. Walter Johnson, 2 vols. (Boston, 1952), 1:481–84.

22. Richard Washburn Child, *A Diplomat Looks at Europe* (New York, 1925), 86. The book includes Child's "Diary at Lausanne."

23. *NYT*, Jan. 7 and 10, 1923; Child, *Diplomat Looks at Europe*, 115; James L. Barton is quoted on the issue in a letter dated May 19, 1922, from Secretary of State Hughes to President Harding, *Foreign Relations of the United States*, 1922 (Washington, D.C., 1928), 2:925.

24. Luther L. Fowle to Ernest W. Riggs, June 10, 1923, in ABC Papers, Central Turkey Mission, 1920–1924, Documents, vol. 1, no. 46; George Sweet Gibb and Evelyn H. Knowlton, *History of the Standard Oil Company: The Resurgent Years, 1911–1927* (New York, 1955), chap. 11. See also John A. DeNovo, *American Interests and Policies in the Middle East, 1900–1939* (Minneapolis, 1963); and Peter H. Buckingham, *International Normalcy: The Open Door Peace with the Former Central Powers, 1921–1929* (Wilmington, Del., 1983).

25. Winston S. Churchill, *The World Crisis: The Aftermath* (London, 1929), 408; Henry Morgenthau, speech at Bowdoin College, quoted in *NYT,* Apr. 24, 1923; Curzon quoted in Derogy, *Resistance and Revenge,* 193; Yves Ternon, *The Armenians: History of a Genocide,* trans. Rouben C. Chalokian (Delmar, N.Y., 1981), 11.

26. William W. Peet to James L. Barton, memorandum, 1923, in ABC Papers, Western Turkey Mission, supp., 1920–24, vol. 1, Documents, no. 37; Barton, "Report on the Lausanne Conference," ibid., no. 328.

27. *Congressional Record,* 67th Cong., 4th sess., 4352.

28. John Hope Simpson, *The Refugee Problem* (London, 1939), 17–21; Henry Morgenthau, *I Was Sent to Athens* (Garden City, N.Y., 1929), chap. 7.

29. Roland Huntford, *Nansen: The Explorer as Hero* (London, 1997), 522; Simpson, *Refugee Problem,* 36–38; *New Near East,* February 1923; Bristol Diary, Aug. 4, 1924.

30. Ernest A. Yarrow, "The Armenian National Problem," *New Near East,* October 1924 and June 1925; *NYT,* July 19, 1926.

31. Fridtjof Nansen, *Armenia and the Near East* (New York, 1976), 35.

32. Ibid., 106–7; Simpson, *Refugee Problem,* chap. 3 and passim.

33. Nansen, *Armenia and the Near East,* 324.

34. *New Near East,* December 1922.

35. Henry H. Riggs, "Standing By the Armenians" (typescript, 1924), in ABC Papers, Turkey and Balkan Missions, supp. vol. 2, no. 283B; William W. Peet to James L. Barton, Aug. 25, 1924, ibid., Western Turkey Mission, vol. 5; and Simpson, *Refugee Problem,* 39, 447–49.

36. Peet to Ernest Riggs, Apr. 13 and Dec. 27, 1923, and Peet to James L. Barton, May 19, 1923, all in ABC Papers, Western Turkey Mission, Letters, 1922–27, vol. 5.

37. *NYT,* Dec. 8, 1924, and Dec. 8, 1925; *New Near East,* January 1924; Charles Vickrey, *International Golden Rule Sunday: A Handbook* (New York, 1926).

38. Riggs, "Standing By the Armenians"; Clair Price quoted in "Mustapha Kemal and the Americans," *Current History* 17 (1922): 117; inscription found in Peet to James L. Barton, Mar. 14, 1923, in ABC Papers, Western Turkey Mission, Letters, 1922–27, vol. 5.

39. Peet to Riggs, Dec. 27, 1923, in ABC Papers, Western Turkey Mission, Letters, vol. 5; Caleb Frank Gates, *Not to Me Only* (Princeton, 1941), chap. 17.

40. Interview notes, Feb. 9, 1923, in William Walker Rockwell Papers, Box 23, Folder 4, New York Public Library; for Harlow, see Horton, *Blight of Asia,* 233–37.

41. *New York Tribune,* Nov. 25, 1923; James W. Gerard, *The Senate Should Reject the Turkish Treaty* (n.p., n.d.) (pamphlet).

42. *NYT,* May 17, 1926; Edward Hale Bierstadt, *The Great Betrayal: A Survey of the Near East Problem* (New York, 1924), 175.

43. Summary of Secretary of State Hughes's speech, Jan. 23, 1924, in *Papers Relating to the Foreign Relations,* 2:409–15; *NYT,* Jan. 24, 1924.

44. Grew, *Turbulent Era,* 1:677.

45. *NYT,* editorial, Jan. 20, 1927.

46. Rose Wilder Lane, "Christmas in Erivan," *Good Housekeeping,* December 1924.
47. NER memorandum, Mar. 10, 1931, Near East Foundation, New York.
48. In addition to the survey, see John S. Badeau and Georgina G. Stevens, *Bread from Stones: Fifty Years of Technical Assistance* (Englewood Cliffs, N.J., 1966).

Epilogue

1. *New Near East,* February 1922.
2. See Robert Mirak's article in *Harvard Encyclopedia of Ethnic Groups,* ed. Stephan Thernstrum (Cambridge, 1980), 36–49; Marion T. Bennett, *American Immigration Policies* (Washington, D.C., 1963); and *Statistical Abstract of the United States,* especially for the years 1930 and 2000.
3. Aghounie Yeghesian, "An Armenian in America," *New Republic,* June 29, 1921, reprinted in *New Near East,* September 1921. Sarkis Atamian, *The Armenian Community* (New York, 1955), provides a good introduction. See also the more recent sociological study: Amy Bakalian, *Armenian-Americans: From Being to Feeling Armenian* (New Brunswick, 1994).
4. See Vigen Guroian, *Faith, Church, Mission: Essays for Renewal in the Armenian Church* (New York, 1995), especially 120–42.
5. Atamian, *Armenian Community,* 366, 358–76.
6. Ibid.; *NYT,* Dec. 25, 1933.
7. Franz Werfel, *The Forty Days of Musa Dagh* (New York, 1934), prefatory note.
8. Ibid., 64. See also Rachel Kirby, *The Culturally Complex Individual: Franz Werfel's Reflections on Minority Identity and Historical Depiction in "The Forty Days of Musa Dagh"* (Lewisburg, Pa., 1999); and Peter S. Jungh, *Franz Werfel,* trans. Anselm Hollo (New York, 1990).
9. Werfel, *Forty Days of Musa Dagh,* 129, 134.
10. Ibid., 817.
11. Harry Boyajian, "Murder Will Out," *Armenian Review* 18 (Fall 1965): 13–14.
12. *New York Times Book Review,* Dec. 2, 1934; Yair Auron, "The Forty Days of Musa Dagh," in *Remembrance and Denial: The Case of the Armenian Genocide,* ed. Richard G. Hovannisian, 47–64 (Detroit, 1998).
13. *NYT,* Aug. 4 and 8, Oct. 30, and Dec. 22, 1945.
14. *NYT,* Mar. 14, 1948, and Jan. 22, 1949; Bakalian, *Armenian-Americans,* 12–14; Hovhannes Mugrditchian, *To Armenians with Love: The Memoirs of a Patriot* (Hobe Sound, Fla., 1996); *NYT,* June 11, 1947.
15. *NYT,* June 2, 1957.
16. See my essay "Responding to the Holocaust," *Virginia Quarterly Review* 75 (Winter 1999): 151–63.
17. See Vahakn N. Dadrian, *The History of the Armenian Genocide: Ethnic Conflict from the Balkans to Anatolia to the Caucasus* (Providence, 1995), 403–4; and in general, Kevord B. Bardakjian, *Hitler and the Armenian Genocide* (Los Angeles, 1985).

18. Bohdan Gebarski quoted in Dickran H. Boyajian, *Armenia: The Case for a Forgotten Genocide* (Westwood, N.J., 1972), 290.

19. *NYT,* Nov. 20, 1967; Apr. 24 and 25, 1965.

20. Marjorie Housepian, "The Unremembered Genocide," *Commentary* 42 (1966): 55–63.

21. *NYT,* Apr. 3 and 14, 1967; "Memorandum of the Armenian National Committee to the Delegates Represented in the U.N. Commission on Human Rights," *Armenian Review* 27 (Summer 1974): 191–203. See also Gerard Libaridian, ed., *A Crime of Silence: The Armenian Genocide; Permanent Peoples' Tribunal* (Totowa, N.J., 1985), 199, 220; and Yves Ternon, *The Armenian Cause,* trans. Anahid Apelian Mangouni (Delmar, N.Y., 1985), 178–81.

22. Hovannisian, *Remembrance and Denial,* 202.

23. *NYT,* May 4, 1975, and May 30, 1977; Libaridian, *Crime of Silence,* 174–75.

24. Marjorie Housepian, *A Houseful of Love* (New York, 1957), 126. For oral history see Donald Miller and Lorna Touryan Miller, *Survivors: An Oral History of the Armenian Genocide* (Berkeley, 1993).

25. Michael Arlen, *Passage to Ararat* (New York, 1975), passim.

26. See Marcus Lee Hansen, *The Problems of the Third Generation Immigrant* (Rock Island, Ill., 1938).

27. For a report of the hearing, see *Armenian Review* 28 (Winter 1976): 339–90.

28. *NYT,* Mar. 1, 1980; *Los Angeles Times,* Jan. 25, 1981.

29. *Los Angeles Times,* Jan. 21 and 28, 1973.

30. Ibid., Jan. 29, Feb. 5 and 16, and Oct. 23, 1982.

31. Libaridian, *Crime of Silence,* passim.

32. *Los Angeles Times,* Apr. 24 and 25, 1983.

33. *Boston Globe,* Apr. 18, 1985.

34. *Los Angeles Times,* May 8, Apr. 25 and 30, 1986.

35. William Saroyan, *The Saroyan Special* (New York, 1948), 13–15, 127.

36. Quoted from William Saroyan, *Here Comes, There Goes, You Know Who* (New York, 1961), in Margaret Bedrosian, *The Magical Pine Ring: Culture and Imagination in Armenian-American Literature* (Detroit, 1991), 149.

37. David Kherdian, *Homage to Adana* (Mt. Horeb, Wis., 1970).

38. Bakalian, *Armenian-Americans,* 65–66.

39. John H. Thompson, *Bob Dole: The Republican Man for All Seasons* (New York, 1994), 182–83; and especially Vigen Guroian, "The Politics and Morality of Genocide," in *The Armenian Genocide: History, Politics, and Ethics,* ed. Richard G. Hovannisian (New York, 1992), 311–39.

40. *NYT,* May 19, 1985. See also Dennis R. Papazian, "Misplaced Credulity: Contemporary Turkish Attempts to Refute the Armenian Genocide," *Armenian Review* 45 (Spring 1992): 185–215.

41. Bernard Lewis, *The Emergence of Modern Turkey* (New York, 1961), 350.

42. Yves Ternon, "Freedom and Responsibility of the Historian: The 'Lewis Affair,'" in Hovannisian, *Remembrance and Denial*, 237–50.

43. *Chronicle of Higher Education*, Oct. 27, 1995; *NYT*, May 22, 1996. See Roger W. Smith, Eric Marcusen, and Robert Jay Lifton, "Professional Ethics and the Denial of the Armenian Genocide," *Holocaust and Genocide Studies* 9, no. 1 (1995): 1–22.

44. *Los Angeles Times*, Dec. 6, 1997.

45. Robert H. Hewsen, *Armenia: A Historical Atlas* (Chicago, 2001), 1.

46. Peter Balakian, *Black Dog of Fate* (New York, 1997), 94–95, 118, 191, 187.

47. "The History of Armenia" appears in Peter Balakian, *June-tree: New and Selected Poems, 1974–2000* (New York, 2001), and also in *Black Dog of Fate*, 184–87.

48. *NYT*, Apr. 12, 2001.

Index

Also by Merrill D. Peterson

The Jefferson Image in the American Mind (1960)
Thomas Jefferson and the New Nation: A Biography (1970)
James Madison: A Biography in His Own Words (1974)
Adams and Jefferson: A Revolutionary Dialogue (1976)
Olive Branch and Sword: The Compromise of 1833 (1982)
The Great Triumvirate: Webster, Clay, and Calhoun (1987)
Lincoln in American Memory (1994)
Coming of Age with the "New Republic," 1938–1950 (1999)
John Brown: The Legend Revisited (2002)

Edited by Merrill D. Peterson

Major Crises in American History (1962), with Leonard Levy
Democracy, Liberty, and Property: State Constitutional Convention Debates of the 1820s
    (1966)
Thomas Jefferson: A Profile (1966)
The Portable Thomas Jefferson (1975)
Thomas Jefferson: Writings (1984)
Thomas Jefferson: A Reference Biography (1986)
The Virginia Statute for Religious Freedom: Its Evolution and Consequences in American History (1988), with Robert Vaughan
Visitors to Monticello (1989)
The Political Writings of Thomas Jefferson (1993)